Two for the Show

scenes for student actors

Brian Kennedy - editor

Playwrights Canada Press
Toronto • Canada

All copyright to the selections and the plays from which they are excerpted are retained by the respective authors.
Two for the Show © Copyright 1999 Brian Kennedy
Playwrights Canada Press
54 Wolseley St., 2nd fl. Toronto, Ontario CANADA M5T 1A5
Tel: (416) 703-0201 Fax: (416) 703-0059
e-mail: orders@puc.ca   http://www.puc.ca

CAUTION: This play is fully protected under the copyright laws of Canada and all other countries of The Copyright Union, and is subject to royalty. Changes to the script are expressly forbidden without the prior written permission of the author. Rights to produce, film, or record, in whole or in part, in any medium or any language, by any group, *amateur or professional*, are retained by the author. To receive information about amateur and professional production rights, contact **Playwrights Union of Canada** at the above addresses.

No part of this book, covered by the copyright hereon, may be reproduced or used in any form or by any means - graphic, electronic or mechanical - without the prior written permission of the *publisher* except for excerpts in a review. Any request for photocopying, recording, taping or information storage and retrieval systems of any part of this book shall be directed in writing to
The Canadian Copyright Licensing Agency, 1 Yonge Street, Suite 1900, Toronto, Ontario CANADA M5E 1E5 tel: (416) 868-1620

Playwrights Canada Press acknowledges the support of The Canada Council for the Arts for our publishing programme
and the Ontario Arts Council.

Cover painting by Shelton Deverell, design by Tony Hamill

Canadian Cataloguing in Publication Data
Main entry under title:
    Two for the Show

ISBN 0-88754-579-3
I. Children's plays, Canadian (English).* 2. Brian Kennedy, 1951
PS8307.T86   1998   .C812'.540809283   C98-932830-9
PR9196.7.C48T86   1998

First edition: March, 1999. Second printing, April 2000.
Printed and bound by Hignell Printing at Winnipeg, Manitoba, Canada.

Two for the Show

Brian Kennedy has enjoyed training and watching high school students take on their first scenes for more than 25 years as a teacher of high school Drama and English in Toronto and Ottawa. *Two for the Show* is the culmination of this experience in four easy sections — the collection he always wished he had.

*To Maureen, Beatrice
and Liam, with love*

Introduction

The aim of this collection is to provide Canadians in their early teens with a selection of two or three character scenes by Canadian playwrights, so that these new actors can learn that the essential process of rehearsing, playing character and staging a short scene is an enjoyable and engaging experience.

So many existing anthologies are set in an adult world, and in the past, leaving these eager with one too many hurdles to cross as they perform for the first time. Cries of, "What does this mean"? and "I can't memorize all this!" would be less frequent if the scene involves settings, themes and characters which are familiar and require little or no explanation, so the new actor can focus on getting the cues and making the lines sound real. Once these essentials are common practice, then new and exotic chords can be introduced and viewed as a challenge.

To further this idea, the collection has been ordered in four sections. Scenes in the first section, ONE - FOR THE MONEY require less time to rehearse, and have fewer **layers** than the scenes of the next section, TWO - FOR THE SHOW, and so on, culminating in the multi-layered challenges of pieces such as "Nurse Jane Goes To Hawaii" in the last section, FOUR - GO, CAT, GO.

Brief introductions at the start of each chapter explain how the actors have "another layer to think about" now, with regard to character, staging, timing, effects, and the like.. Each section attempts to offer a balance of male/female roles, comic and dramatic scenes and always favours the **two-hander** over multiple role scenes. (Scenes noted as **3 roles**, etc., can be played by males or females.) Lastly, there are enough scenes in each section to monitor the progress of an entire class, section by section.

Now, go, cat, go!

To The Teacher

As a high school drama teacher, I have searched for twenty odd years for a scene text that would satisfy the particular demands of the first year Drama student, which in Ontario can mean either Grades 8, 9, 10 or 11. The biggest numbers occur in Drama in these grades, particularly the first year of high school as students take their 'Arts Credit', and yet, I've searched in vain for a simple scene text for classroom performances which would teach the basics without a great deal of memory work, set building or explanation.

Yes, there are many excellent scene anthologies out there, but they all have scripts aimed at more experienced, senior students, both in content and in language. The junior drama student needs more here and now, more teen characters and situations, most of all, more comedy.

I think I've found them. And they are all written by Canadians. As a matter of fact, like most good discoveries, they were right in front of me all along. I've been using the plays of marvellous writers like John Lazarus and Dennis Foon for years as senior class touring shows and festival pieces, but to imagine them chopped up as short scenes for junior classes — surely they wouldn't hold up under the jaded eye of a fourteen-year old? What was I thinking? Even in short bursts, writers like these know fourteen year olds as well as their teachers. They know teenage concerns; they know the sound of their conversations; they know what makes them laugh.

Then, I made a second discovery. Most of the playwrights in the table of contents, had their *first* pieces published in the 1970's. Coincidence? Ah-ha! While the rest of us have been learning how to teach, they've been mastering the art of writing plays for Young People's Theatre; the demographics of the theatre community and the baby boom have conspired to give Canada the same flowering of original theatre for youth in the 1990's, as the adult theatre boom experienced in the early 1970's. Cobble all this YPT talent with a number of exciting new playwrights (like Ragna Leanna Goodwin), season with some old favourites of the adult stage, such as George F. Walker, Allan Stratton and Carol Shields, and I think we have a winner. Enjoy.

A NOTE ON THEORY: In the course of introducing each of the 39 scenes, I've attempted to introduce some of the vocabulary of the stage into student conversation. Many of these terms, says my thirteen year old, 'everybody knows' already. Fine. I've explained most terms (in **bold**) such as **aside** and **doubling** as I went, but I suggest, that as a teacher, you devise a few lessons on the more difficult ideas of **comic stereotypes** or **sub-text** to ensure comprehension (even though everybody knows what they mean already).

A NOTE ON THE NEWEST THEORY: In Ontario, secondary school reform has produced several 'Draft' documents on drama education in 1998. Drama at the Grade 9 level will be offered, starting September 1999, as an 'Open' single credit course, and/or as a portion of a 'Comprehensive' Arts credit. Grade 10 Drama will be offered as a single credit, 'Open' course. (Other credit courses in Drama are encouraged, but these are the 'core' courses.)

How does this anthology suit these needs? Quite nicely, I think. *The Secondary Policy Draft for the Arts, Grades 9 and 10* (Ontario Ministry of Education, Toronto, October 1998) specifically recommends that "In grade 9, students work with material from a wide range of authors, categories and cultures" and that student work "broadens to encompass theatrical conventions and techniques." (*Secondary Policy Draft*, p. 2)

This anthology offers a wide exposure to different playwrights, a variety of cultural and social settings, and introduces the essential conventions and vocabulary of the stage.

A NOTE ON EVALUATION: At time of publication, the Ontario Ministry appeared to favour a four-level, four-category 'rubric' model for evaluation of students in the Arts. The division of the anthology itself into four sections offers an evaluation template which could be used to assess student progress. Any one of the scenes could be performed at a Level 4, but scenes in sections One and Two may also be assessed as requiring a lower achievement level to perform well than those in the last two sections. Moreover, the outcomes of individual performances of *any* scene could, of course, be assessed along the lines of the Ministry guide using a simple 'rubric', such as the one suggested below, developed in collaboration with a Grade 9 Drama class before they performed *their* scenes. Listening to student expectations for performance before deciding on rubric terms — making the tool collaborative — is always a rewarding activity for both teacher and student. Such a scale would also have to be adjusted according to whether this particular presentation of the scene in question was the first or final one by the students, and from which chapter of this text, or level or difficulty and challenge, the scene is taken.

Sample performance rubric

MARK	LINES	CONCENTRATION	VOICE
1	needed prompts to continue	very little concentration	spoke only to partner, words not clear to audience
2	no prompts but miscues, missing lines, hesitation	showed emotion, character, but lost concentration	low volume or articulation made hearing difficult
3	word for word lines and cues	good concentration emotions clear	volume and articulation adequate for room
4	perfect lines, cues skillfully timed	excellent concentration and created credible character and emotional transitions	every word clearly, easily heard anywhere in the room

And, finally, to the teacher of English...

Although your students may be less enthusiastic than a drama class about performing these scenes (then again, you may be surprised), they also offer an excellent introduction to **playwriting** and **critical analysis of dramatic text**.

Creating **dialogue** beyond the, "I'm fine. Has it been raining long?" school of writing is always a challenge. The basics are all here: dialogue motivated by character and action (rather than the weather), and essential **dramatic terms** crisis, climax, contrasting characters, comedy, farce, melodrama, comedy noir, play within a play, to name a few.

As well, relevant themes for discussion and writing abound: feminism (INDIRA AND SHARON from "Carrying in the Calf") or MARI'S BOYFRIEND from "Body Image Project"), immigration (LO, NICKNICK from "New Canadian Kid"), suicide ("Donne In"), colonialism (FIGHTER PILOT from "Billy Bishop Goes To War"), alcoholism (JACE from "Liars"), and social values ("We'll Be Fine"). There is also many themes, such as relationships, that run through a number of different scenes, from the destructive (QUINN'S ADVICE - "Body Image Project"), to the downright humourous (ALPHA AND BETA - "Arrivals and Departures"), to the destructive *and* humourous ("Sibyl and Sylvia"). I'm sure you can find more. Break a leg.

To the Actor

If you try different voices or characters in front of the mirror (and more courageously in front of your friends) or, if you are the kind of person who likes to practice something new until you get it right, then you should find acting the scenes in this book enjoyable. Having a memorized script, and a planned series of moves and reactions, makes your scene even more funny, or moving, or both, and brings you closer to the lives of the audience. Their applause when you finish will tell you that you've done a good job of communicating just what *you* liked about this character and scene in the first place.

But first, rehearse — so you and your partner can get it right. Here's a rehearsal plan that works — try it.

First, find out what kind of character you want to play by reading the short descriptions before each scene in this section. Then do a **read-through** with your partner(s), trying to get your character's voice and emotion right.

As you read, note if your scene is set in one location and over one continuous period of time. Most are. If it is, you don't have to plan any blackouts or scene changes, so just figure out what, and where, the major set pieces, or **properties**, (**props**) are and place chairs or boxes on your stage to represent them. If your scene needs a **hand prop**, like a phone, make sure it's on stage when you begin. A simple sketch, a drawing of the stage viewed from above, helps both actors to agree on the set beforehand. If your scene is more complex in terms of time or setting, then you will have to plan a different part of the stage for a different time or place. Try to avoid using blackouts — they interrupt the scene — let the audience use their imaginations too.

Next, do a **walk-through** with your script in hand to know when you **enter** and **exit**. Audiences get bored with characters who don't move during a scene, so plan some **blocking**, or stage movement, to create some life to the scene or to underline how your character is feeling at one particular moment. This is true even if your characters are in a restaurant, for example, or in the school cafeteria — sit *on* the table, if it's in character — or at least make some **gestures** to help convey the emotions in the scene.

Now, the only thing between you and performance are all those lines. Sit with your partner(s) and do a **line rehearsal**. Memorizing lines is like eating pizza — do it one section at a time, not all at once. A new 'section', or **beat**, begins when a new idea or emotion appears, or when one character enters or exits. Underline key words in your lines as a memory aid.

When you can leave your script aside, even for one **beat**, rehearse the scene **off-book**, that is, with nobody looking at their lines (no cheating!). When you can all do this for the whole scene — you're done! Get an audience.

Note that throughout the book, drama terms have been printed in **bold**. If you don't understand what a particular term means from the context, ask your teacher. Please also note that some scenes do not have a SCENE TITLE, such as SIDEKICK from "Dreaming and Duelling". These works are actually short plays complete unto themselves and not excerpted from longer works — for example: "Sibyl and Sylvia" by Colleen Currran and "Derailed" by Emil Sher.

ACKNOWLEDGMENTS: I'd like to thank colleagues Mac Dodge of the Niagara District School Board, and Michael Wilson of the Ottawa Carleton District School Board for their advice and encouragement in the preparation of this anthology.

I would also like to express my heartfelt appreciation to Tony Hamill for his knowledge, expertise, and invaluable advice in preparation of this book.

Finally, a big thanks to Angela Rebeiro of Playwrights Canada Press for her ideas, advice and support, and for several wonderful conversations on drama, education and teens.

Table of Contents

Section One - ONE FOR THE MONEY

1. "The Girl's Room" *by R. L. Goodwin*   (2F)   p. 2

2. Victor and Rocky   (2M)
   "Secrets" *by John Lazarus*   p. 7

3. Mari's Boyfriend   (2F/1M)
   "The Body Image Project" *by Eleanor Albamese*   p. 11

4. Blue Jays   (2M)
   "The Bar Mitzvah Speech" *by J.J. Steinfeld*   p. 17

5. "Plans" *by Brian Kennedy*   (2F)   p. 22

6. Hangin' at the Handy   (3 roles)
   "Video Wars" *by Rex Deverell*   p. 27

7. Quinn's Advice   (2F/1M)
   "The Body Image Project" *by Eleanor Albanese*   p. 32

8. Katie   (2F/1M)
   "Yellow on Thursdays" *by Sara Graefe*   p. 38

9. Jennifer's Story   (4 roles)
   "Weird Kid" *by Rex Deverell*   p. 43

10. Barbie and Ken   (1F/1M)
    "That's No Lady, that's My Immigrant!"
    by Sandra Dempsey   p. 50

Section Two - Two for the Show

11. Mr Lizard (1F/1M or 1F)
"Skin" *by Dennis Foon* *p. 58*

12. Fantasy Date (2F/1M)
"Thin Ice" *by Banuta Rubess, Beverley Cooper* *p. 62*

13. "Robbie's Secret" *by Brian Kennedy* (2M) *p. 67*

14. Purple Face (1F/1M)
"Dreaming and Duelling"
by John Lazarus & Joa Lazarus *p. 72*

15. Phiroza and Todd (1F/1M)
"Skin" *by Dennis Foon* *p. 77*

16. Indie (2F)
"Carrying the Calf" *by Shirley Barrie* *p. 82*

17. "Derailed" *by Emil Sher* (2M) *p. 89*

18. Alpha and Beta (2 roles)
"Departures and Arrivals" *by Carol Shields* *p. 94*

19. The Proposal (1F/1M)
"1837: The Farmer's Revolt" *by Rick Salutin* *p. 99*

20. Total Commitment (2F)
"Secrets" *by John Lazarus* *p. 103*

21. Jace (2M)
"Liars" *by Dennis Foon* *p. 109*

22. Penthouse Magazine (2F/2M)
"Thin Ice" *by Banuta Rubess, Beverley Cooper* *p. 114*

23. Cool (1F/1M)
"Secrets" *by John Lazarus* *p. 120*

SECTION THREE - THREE TO GET READY

24. "Solo" *by Irene N. Watts* (2F) *p. 128*

25. I'VE DONE IT (2M)
"Secrets" *by John Lazarus* *p. 135*

26. TRUTH (1F/1M)
"Liars" *by Dennis Foon* *p. 142*

27. ...OR DARE (1F/1M)
"Liars" *by Dennis Foon* *p. 150*

28. EVERYBODY'S DIFFERENT (2F/1M)
"Yellow on Thursdays" *by Sara Graefe* *p. 157*

29. "Buster" *by R. L. Goodwin* (1F/1M) *p. 168*

30. "Don't Call Me That" *by Alica Payne* (1F/2M) *p. 173*

31. THE MASTER CRIMINAL (2M)
"Zastrozzi" *by George F. Walker* *p. 182*

32. LO, NICKNICK (1F/1M)
"New Canadian Kid" *by Dennis Foon* *p. 187*

33. FIGHTER PILOT (2M)
"Billy Bishop Goes to War"
by John Gray, Eric Peterson *p. 194*

SECTION FOUR - GO, CAT GO!

34. "Sibyl and Sylvia" *by Colleen Curran* (2F) *p. 202*

35. "Donne In" *by Yvette Nolan* (2M) *p. 214*

36. "I Am Marguerite" *by Shirley Barrie* (2F) *p. 223*

37. PASSION AND DESIRE (1F/1M)
"Nurse Jane Goes to Hawaii" *by Allan Stratton* *p. 229*

38. "We'll by Fine" *by Irene N. Watts* (2F) *p. 242*

39. SIDEKICK (2M)
"Dreaming and Duelling"
by John Lazarus & Joa Lazarus *p. 251*

Section One — ONE FOR THE MONEY

There are some really juicy roles in these short scenes. And, since most scenes in this section is set in one location and over one continuous period of time, you don't have to plan blackouts or scene changes; just follow the rehearsal plan previously outlined.

If you've ever sweated it out before asking a guy to dance, try the role of Anna from "The Girl's Room". Or, check out how Victor, "the Boa Constrictor", gets some timely advice on condoms from Rocky in VICTOR AND ROCKY ("Secrets"). Want more action than words? Try HANGIN' AT THE HANDY ("Video Wars") for lots of movement and pace.

Another 'tough guy' role, only not as nice as Rocky's character at all, is Quinn in the scene subtitled MARI'S BOYFRIEND and again in QUINN'S ADVICE (both from "The Body Image Project"). This role takes a lot of concentration to play well — he's scary. So do the comic roles in KEN AND BARBIE ("That's No Lady, That's My Immigrant!"), although this scene is easy to memorize, you have to stay focused and don't laugh at yourselves — that's the audience's role.

Here are the scenes in this section. Check out individual intros for more ... break a leg.

Scene 1

"The Girl's Room"

by R.L. Goodwin

2 females

    Ragna Leanna Goodwin began writing scenes in high school. She now is a 24-year-old graduate of Queen's University and writes poetry, short stories and plays from her home in Peterborough. She's a versatile writer. Her second scene in this collection. "Buster", (Scene 29), is written in a completely different style.

    Anna and Melanie are not alike — this tension is what makes the scene 'work'. Try to show the audience the difference in their personalities in your movements and gestures as well as in your voice. You know people like this!

    Notice that Anna enters first. Have the actor playing Melanie give her partner some time alone on stage, before Melanie enters, to show the audience how Anna is feeling as she looks at herself in the mirror.

    Finally, the short "mistaken/mistook" **beat** (a section of the dialogue that deals with one idea or emotion) is more than just a grammar lesson. See if you can communicate the double meaning in those lines by using emphasis, or **inflection**, in the right places, on the right words.

The Girl's Room

The curtain opens on the inside of a girl's washroom. Typical layout for a public facility. The play takes place sometime in the evening during a high school dance. Faint music can be heard throughout. becoming more pronounced when the door swings open.

The first girl enters and heads straight for the mirror. She looks at herself, shaking her head in apparent disgust. The second girl enters.

MELANIE	Why are you hiding in the bathroom?
ANNA	I'm not hiding; I'm ... glossing.
MELANIE	You glossed five minutes ago.
ANNA	Well, I'm doing it again!
MELANIE	If you don't ask him to dance soon, I'll do it for you.
ANNA	No! Don't you dare!
MELANIE	Then go out there and ask him!
ANNA	I will ... later.
MELANIE	Anna!
ANNA	Oh Melanie, I just can't! What if he says no? Oh God, I'd die!
MELANIE	And if he says yes?

ANNA (*blissfully*) Oh God, I'd die. (*shakes her head and frowns*) Look, both scenarios are resulting in a fatality. I think it would be best for me to just remain in the bathroom—

MELANIE Anna, this is your youth! These are the best years of your life. You cannot spend the duration of your adolescence curled up in a fetal position next to the tampon dispenser'

ANNA But I'm not like you, Melly! I can't ... talk to guys.

MELANIE Nonsense. Of course you can.

ANNA No, I can't. I get all flustered and start dropping things. I can never think of anything to say and I wind up just standing there looking stupid...

MELANIE Well, better out there than in here! At least if you leave the bathroom there is a remote chance you might be mistaken for someone normal.

ANNA Mistook.

MELANIE What?

ANNA I think it's mistook, not mistaken.

MELANIE Mistaken is a word!

ANNA Yes, I know, but I think you've used it incorrectly.

MELANIE No, mistaken is the term that is used to indicate the present tense, for example "If she thinks she's going to distract me from the subject at hand, she is very much mistaken." Mistook is the term which applies when using the past tense.

Two for the Show / 5

ANNA · For example "She mistook me for someone who cared."?

MELANIE · Exactly.

ANNA · (*sarcastically*) Well, then I'm all set! I can just go on out there and dazzle him with my grammar!

MELANIE · Syntax. Grammar is ...

ANNA · (*warning her*) I'm going to hurt you...

MELANIE · The only one you're hurting here, is yourself.

ANNA · And exactly how am I doing that?

MELANIE · By being so caught up in every bad thing that might happen, you're denying yourself the possibility of anything good happening!

ANNA · I'd rather not be remembered at all, then be remembered as the girl that made a fool of herself.

MELANIE · If that were really true, I don't think you would have bothered to come tonight.

ANNA · I'm beginning to wonder why I did.

MELANIE · Just in case.

ANNA · Just in case what?

MELANIE · Exactly. It's the "just in case's" in life that keep us going.

ANNA · I don't know...

MELANIE · I'll tell you something. It's a lot easier to live with embarrassment than it is to live with regret.

ANNA   I see. And just when did you become so worldly and wise?

MELANIE   I've spent a fair amount of time in the Girl's Room.

ANNA   *(sighing dramatically)* All right. Let's get this over with.

              The two girls start to walk off stage.

              I'll ask him.

MELANIE   What are you, crazy? You'll make a fool of yourself...

                            * * *

Scene 2

from "Secrets"

by John Lazarus

2 males

VICTOR AND ROCKY

Very few Canadian playwrights have the experience and skill of John Lazarus. He has worked for over twenty-five years in theatre, much of it in theatre for youth. Rocky, Victor, Susan and Binnie are all characters from his one act comic drama called "Secrets". There are more scenes from "Secrets" elsewhere in the collection. It makes an excellent class production.

In this scene you can see how quickly the writer establishes two very different characters within a **comic scenario**. Rocky has too much of a reputation with girls, and Victor is trying desperately to establish one. Use **body language** and **facial reactions**, not just dialogue, to show the audience the big difference between these two guys..

Notice how Rocky talks directly to the audience in his first speech, before Victor enters. This technique is called **direct address**, and allows the writer to further his theme by using Rocky as a narrator as well as a character in the scene. Where have you seen this done before? On TV? In a movie? A turn, a gesture, or a change in voice after he finishes the opening speech, will help the audience enjoy Rocky's **transition** from talking to the audience, to then pretending they are not there.

Victor and Rocky

> *The setting is the front porch of VICTOR's house during a party. ROCKY, widely admired as a stud, is feeling guilty about having deceived his girlfriend, who is starting to suspect. VICTOR, widely thought of as gay, is finally getting somewhere with Susan, the girl he has a crush on.*

ROCKY | (*enters, addresses audience*) So now she's stopped dancing with that moron, and she's sitting in a corner of the room pretending to neck with him. But all the time she keeps sneakin' these little glances at me. With that look that she gets instead of crying an' screaming. I never know how to play these kinds of games. Gimme two teams, a ball an' a scoreboard any day. (*as VICTOR enters*) Yo, it's the Boa Constrictor. How's your date goin'?

VICTOR | Wonderful. Wonderful. Absolutely wonderful.

ROCKY | Yeah, I hear you an' Susan are makin' out.

VICTOR | Well, I wouldn't put it like — well, yeah.

ROCKY | Congratulations. Ya got protection?

VICTOR | Oh, don't you start this stuff about Susan.

ROCKY | It has nothin' to do with the garbage about Susan. It's with everybody. Gotta play safe, man.

VICTOR | Look, it would be great, and who knows, maybe some day. But that's not what tonight is about, okay?

ROCKY	Okay. Chill. I'm just sayin', would you rather have one an' not need it, or need one an' not have it?
VICTOR	Oh. Yeah. Good point.
ROCKY	You don't got none, do you?
VICTOR	Well, I don't keep 'em in the house 'cause I don't want my sister or my mom finding them, and I didn't buy any today 'cause I didn't want Susan to think I was that kind of a guy, or to think that I think she's that kind of a girl—
ROCKY	Hey! This is the Nineties, Victor, this is life or death!
VICTOR	Yeah and if my mom found them it would be.
ROCKY	What about your ol' man? Does he have any?
VICTOR	My father? What for?
ROCKY	For makin' balloon animals, what do you *think* for? How can such a smart guy be such a feeb? Why don't you go look, just in case?
VICTOR	*Steal* my *father's* condoms? Do you have any idea how Freudian that is?
ROCKY	So you wanna borrow from me, is that it?
VICTOR	Well, if you insist. Just in case.
ROCKY	(*taking from his pocket*) I got three. Here, take 'em.
VICTOR	All of 'em? What about you?
ROCKY	Don't need 'em any more. I'm quitting.
VICTOR	You're what?

ROCKY   Givin' up on women. Gonna be a monk.

Gives him the condoms.

VICTOR   We gotta talk about this, okay? Not right now, but soon, okay?

ROCKY   Hey, man. Be good to her.

VICTOR   I really don't think it's gonna happen tonight, Rocky.

ROCKY   I didn't say that. I just said, be good to her.

VICTOR   I will. Thanks. Later.

VICTOR exits to the house. ROCKY stays on the porch and broods.

***

Scene 3

from "The Body Image Project"

by Eleanor Albanese

2 females / 1 male

MARI'S BOYFRIEND

Eleanor Albanese has written plays that have toured hundreds of schools in Ontario. She also has taught Theatre Arts at university and college level, published short stories and co-founded a theatre company in her home town of Thunder Bay. And, she's a writer who's not afraid to tackle important issues.

This is the first of two scenes, both in this section, about Mari, Quinn, her popular girlfriend, and Mari's new boyfriend, David. As you will see from his first moments on stage, David is very demanding and possessive. Most girls would dump him *during* the first date, but not Mari. As she tells Quinn "You've had lots of boyfriends. This is the first time a guy's even looked at me." For this reason, Mari is a tough role. She desperately wants David to like her, but she doesn't want to become his complete slave either. A good actor will show this inner struggle.

Another moment that needs practice is, of course, the kiss. Really, it's not a kiss, but a near miss, because Mari deftly escapes David's advance. Rehearse any **stage romance** as you would a dance, or a stage fight for that matter, by choreographing — numbering — each move.

Finally, this scene needs a set change. Probably the easiest way is **split stage**, that is, show Quinn on the phone at her house by placing her under one light **downstage right or left**, and simply have this small part of the stage go dim after the call is over. Character turmoil, a choreographed kiss and a light cue — can you remember all this and your lines too? This one's a challenge.

Mari's Boyfriend

MARI's livingroom.

MARI (*answering the phone*) Hello?

QUINN Hi, it's me.

MARI Oh, hi Quinn.

QUINN You seeing David tonight?

MARI Quinn, I told you, don't say his name over the phone. My Mom listens in on my phone calls.

QUINN (*in a sing-song voice*) Mrs. Slovane, are you there?

MARI She's gone out. (*putting on a pair of earrings as she talks*)

QUINN So do you and "bleep" want to meet us at Pizza Hut.

MARI I kind of already ate.

QUINN So just have coffee.

MARI I should check with David first. He gets weird if I plan something without telling him.

QUINN Do you have to get permission for everything?

MARI No but I have a feeling we were supposed to go to this party tonight.

QUINN With his friends, of course.

MARI	I can't help it if he's older than us. I mean, he doesn't want to hang around with kids younger than him.
QUINN	Right, that wouldn't be cool.
MARI	Quinn, I haven't been going out with him that long. I just don't want to blow it, alright? You've had lots of boyfriends. This is the first time a guy's even looked at me.
QUINN	Yeah right. Well, I guess I'll see you at school tomorrow.
MARI	Quinn, you and I'll do something together this week. I promise. Okay?
QUINN	Sure, no problem.

There's a knock at MARI's door.

MARI	There's someone at my door. I gotta go.
QUINN	Me too. Bye.
MARI	See ya.

DAVID walks right in.

MARI	David, what are you doing here? My Dad would kill me if he saw you here.
DAVID	No one's going to touch you while I'm around.
MARI	You have to go. I'll meet you in ten minutes downtown.
DAVID	Relax. (*starts walking around the livingroom*) Nice place. Your parents rich or something?
MARI	No, they just both work. David—
DAVID	Where's your old man?

MARI	Him and my Mom are out. But I don't know when they'll be back.
DAVID	Let me get this straight. Your mom and your dad are out?
MARI	Yes, but they could be...
DAVID	And where'd you say your brother was?
MARI	Work.
DAVID	Alright. (*sitting down*) We've got the place to ourselves. Come here.
MARI	(*not moving*) But my parents—
DAVID	You worry too much. If we hear your parents drive up, I'll do my disappearing act. You've got a back door, don't you?
MARI	Yes, but I thought we were going to a party tonight.
DAVID	It's early. Relax. Come here. I'm not going to bite you. I just thought, you know, we have a little privacy, we could talk, get close.
MARI	We could talk outside.
DAVID	Mari, Mari, Mari. I am your boyfriend, correct?
MARI	Yes. I mean, we're going out.
DAVID	Well... What planet are you from — Mars? Sit down.
	MARI reluctantly sits beside him. DAVID begins playing with her hair.
DAVID	Where'd you get the earrings?

MARI	They're Quinn's.
DAVID	A little wild, don't you think?
MARI	I don't know. Do you like my jeans? I just got them.
DAVID	Nice. Stand up. Turn around.
	MARI stands up and turns around for DAVID to see the jeans.
DAVID	Very nice.
	MARI sits back down beside him. He starts to kiss her. He moves towards her as if to move on top of her. She slides off the chair and he lands face first onto the arm of the chair.
DAVID	You trying to make a fool out of me? Nobody makes a fool out of me.
MARI	David no. I just — I want to go slow, that's all. And I'm scared my parents are...
DAVID	You're full of it, you know that? You know what I think? I think the only reason you're going out with me is to look good with your friends.
MARI	That's not true.
DAVID	I'm talking here, okay? Ah, forget it. This isn't worth it. Where's my coat?
	MARI quickly gets DAVID's coat from where he dropped it on the floor.
MARI	Do you want me to go with you?
DAVID	Just give it to me. (*grabs the coat and starts to leave*)

MARI   David, wait— I—

DAVID   Tell someone who cares.

             DAVID exits.

                    * * *

Scene 4

from "The Bar Mitzvah Speech"

by J.J. Steinfeld

2 males

BLUE JAYS

Actors are polymaths. That is, because they have to research so many different roles, histories, languages as part of their job, they know a lot about a very wide variety of topics. (This is also why they are also so much fun at a party!) This scene may add some new words to your knowledge and broaden your experience as an actor, and as a person.

In the Jewish religion, a Bar Mitzvah is the ceremony during which a thirteen-year-old boy becomes "a man". In this scene, Joel is a day away from his Bar Mitzvah and Noah, his serious, nineteen-year-old brother has come to Joel's room to help him memorize his speech for the *shul*, or synagogue. Joel is a Toronto Blue Jays fanatic — he'd rather be batting for his team, or watching the Jays on TV, than studying. To get him more serious about his values, Noah, who studies psychology and is on the debating team at university and is *very* serious, has given Joel the book to which they refer.

J.J. Steinfeld, a Charlottetown creator of short stories and plays, has written a scene that is familiar territory to anyone who has an older brother who feels he must assume the role of parent to his younger sibling now and then. Noah has good intentions, and Joel eventually goes along with them (albeit after a little well-chosen threat on Noah's part).

This scene has many **hand props**. Joel's bat, ball, cap and glove, his skullcap (or yarmulke), and the typed speech. You might even use two books to represent a copy of the Torah, the Jewish 'bible', and the book Noah loans Joel. Get these items and learn how to use them in rehearsal to give the scene movement — a good actor can use a baseball bat to show how his character is feeling as well as a fine swing. And, don't forget to place them exactly where you want them on stage.

Blue Jays

	It is about fifteen minutes since JOEL has gone to his bedroom. Stage left is illuminated, JOEL's bedroom. NOAH is standing by the bed in the centre of the bedroom, with a typed copy of the Bar Mitzvah speech and a white skullcap in his hand. JOEL is standing near him, wearing his good suit, Blue Jays cap, and with his tie around his neck untied. His baseball uniform, glove, bat, and ball are on the unmade bed. NOAH is casually dressed.
NOAH	*(putting down the speech and skullcap on the bed, he helps to tie his brother's tie)* You don't look half bad.
JOEL	*(grimacing)* Why do I have to wear my suit now?
NOAH	This is a full dress rehearsal. It's for real tomorrow morning.
JOEL	I can wear my baseball uniform and practise just as well.
NOAH	I want to create the mood for tomorrow. A person acts differently when he's dressed differently. Elementary psychology, little brother. *(finishing off tying the tie)*
JOEL	You take too many psychology courses.
NOAH	I enjoy psychology. I use what I learn in psychology for debating ... and for life, in general.

JOEL	(*taking a batting swing at a phantom pitch after NOAH walks away from him*) It would be great to wear my baseball uniform in the synagogue. The rabbi could pitch.
NOAH	(*picking up the speech and skullcap from the bed*) One Bar Mitzvah a lifetime, and you're determined to sabotage yours.
JOEL	I'll be fantastic tomorrow. (*he takes another swing*) I'm going to hit a home run... (*one more swing, then using his sportscaster's voice*) Going ... going ... gone over the centre field fence for a grand-slam homer by Joel Resnick.
	NOAH removes his brother's Blue Jays cap and tosses it onto the bed and then tries to put the skullcap on his brother's moving head.
NOAH	Hold still...
JOEL	(*returning to his regular voice*) Leave my head alone, Noah.
NOAH	You'll have to wear a yarmulke tomorrow.
JOEL	Then I'll wear it tomorrow.
NOAH	We're pretending it's tomorrow.
JOEL	You put on my yarmulke. It'll keep your brains warm.
NOAH	It's your brains I'm concerned about.
JOEL	Where does it say you can't wear a Blue Jays cap to get Bar Mitzvahed? Where, huh?
NOAH	In the Torah.
JOEL	What a big liar. (*puts on his Blue Jays cap again*)

NOAH (*waving the skullcap at his brother*) If you'd read your Torah a little more and your baseball books and magazines a little less, maybe you'd know that.

JOEL The Torah says that big debating brothers with big debating brains should be nicer to their little brothers.

NOAH In the same section where it prohibits wearing baseball caps in synagogue?

JOEL (*adjusting his cap*) A Blue Jays cap and a yarmulke are pretty close.

NOAH (*grabbing the Blue Jays cap and forcing the skullcap on his brother's head*) Pretend it is tomorrow, Joel, all right?

NOAH tosses the cap onto the bed.

JOEL Well, where's my audience? I don't see the fans.

NOAH (*extending his right hand over the room*) They're all here. The place is packed. SkyDome as *shul*. You're in your element, Joel.

JOEL You going to sell kosher hot dogs?

NOAH I'm going to listen to your melodious voice. Run through the speech the way you're going to do it in the synagogue. (*adjusts the skullcap securely on his brother's head*)

JOEL Don't you want to discuss Jean-Paul Sartre's *Anti-Semite and Jew* first?

NOAH You're not going to tell me you've read the book since this afternoon.

JOEL A few pages.

NOAH	I hope you're starting to understand why those words you used are wrong.
JOEL	I'm not completely dense. I do try to learn from my mistakes.
NOAH	(*smiling*) There's hope for you yet.
JOEL	Let's rehearse later. I'm not in the mood.
NOAH	We're going to rehearse now... (*looking at the sheet of paper in his hand*) I'm not leaving this room until I hear you do the speech right.
JOEL	I want to go play some baseball. I need to get to the field early so I can work on my hitting.
NOAH	I should have known that's why you don't want to rehearse.
JOEL	And the Blue Jays game is going to be on TV later. I'll probably miss four or five innings, but we're having a game also.
NOAH	Dad won't let you watch unless I tell him you know your speech *perfectly*.
JOEL	(*speaking rapidly*) Worthy Rabbi, holy congregation, beloved parents, my brother, precious Grandmother...

* * *

Scene 5

"Plans"

by Brian Kennedy

2 females

For every role you play, you should have a clear idea of what your character wants from others, from herself, or even from life. Actors call this, finding the character's **intention,** and it will help you find the right emotion for the lines.

Just to be a nuisance, I wrote this scene to show how a character's intention can change! At first, Diana wants her mother to listen and understand her situation. When her mother refuses to change her attitude, Diana's intention changes — she shows a new side to her character. Two-sided characters are always more realistic and more appealing to an audience than one dimensional ones, like Mom.

For the actor who plays Caroline, however, there is a different challenge. *Don't* be tempted to play her as a **comic stereotype** of the evil mom — that's not the way the scene was written. Try to make the audience see her *good* side too, although you'll have to use gestures and reactions to do so, since the lines, I admit, make her pretty mean.

Plans

>*DIANA seventeen, three months pregnant, in shorts and a T-shirt. CAROLINE her mother, fashionably dressed.*
>
>*In the local pizza restaurant. DIANA and her mother enter. CAROLINE looks uncomfortable — she's a little too well dressed for this place. They sit at the first table.*

CAROLINE: It was so nice of you to bring me to lunch, Diana. You are just full of surprises.

DIANA: Yes, I am.

CAROLINE: You mean you have more?

DIANA: No, just kidding (*a feeble laugh*). I just thought that we could "do lunch" the way you're always going out with your friends at work. Maybe talk a bit.

CAROLINE: Well, that was very thoughtful, dear. But, offering to buy as well. Are you sure you don't want me to....

DIANA: No, Mom. I have the money. Just relax and ... enjoy yourself.

CAROLINE: Well, isn't that grown-up!

DIANA: (*reacts, then seeing waiter*) Here's the waiter, let's get something to eat.

>*They order. The waiter returns with the food later in the scene.*

CAROLINE: This isn't about university, is it, dear? You know your father and I have sacrificed a great deal to save enough for your degree,

	and would be awfully disappointed if you continued with this hairdressing idea. You have many years ahead of you, Diana. Don't throw them away on some foolish mistake.
DIANA	I don't want to throw anything away. It's just that sometimes ... things just don't go the way you've planned. Did that ever happen to you? Was there ever a time for you when your life took a different direction than the one you had in mind?
CAROLINE	This is about university, isn't it? You have decided to waste your time on some silly scheme. Think about your future, Diana. I know you don't realize it now, but you will spend a great deal of time working at whatever career you chose — you have a long life after graduation.
DIANA	I am thinking about my future, believe me.
CAROLINE	That's great, dear! I'll tell Dad what you've decided as soon as he gets back from his business trip. Which university and programme have you decided on?
DIANA	(*aside*) Oh, god. (*to CAROLINE*) I mean, good, the food's here! I'm starving!
CAROLINE	Dear, you changed the subject.
DIANA	Smells good, doesn't it?
CAROLINE	I know you well enough, that you never do anything without a plan. So, what is it, dear, why have you brought me here?
DIANA	Well, Mom, I...
CAROLINE	If it isn't university, then it must be Joe. I've hardly seen you all summer because of him. Don't get to involved, Diana. You're still so young.

DIANA   Mom, you're always talking to me about the future, about my future. About having plans and following them through...

CAROLINE   Well, if you want something in life, you have to have a plan and stick to it.

DIANA   But, does everything have to follow a plan? Sometimes life can't be so ...

CAROLINE   Yes, but if you plan first, then you will succeed.

DIANA   No, Mom. Sometimes plans go wrong, and it's not your fault. Joe and I...

CAROLINE   What's Joe got to do with this. It's your life we're talking about, not his.

DIANA   He's a part of my life.

CAROLINE   He's just a summer boyfriend, Diana. You're seventeen. You've got years ahead of you for boyfriends and serious relationships. (*pause*) How serious is Joe?

DIANA   Real serious.

CAROLINE   What do you mean?

DIANA   Mom, I'm going to have a baby.

CAROLINE   (*reacts*) Oh, Diana, no! What on earth,...? Are you ... sure?

DIANA   Yes, I am. I'm sure. I've been to a doctor. I'm three months ... pregnant. Joe's the father. He knows. He says he'll ...

CAROLINE   This is a fine mess. How do you think your father will react? What were you thinking?

DIANA   That's just it, Mom, I wasn't. Thinking. There was no plan. It just happened. Joe thinks ...

CAROLINE	I don't care what Joe thinks. He's done just about enough, thank you very much!
DIANA	We're in this together, Mom. Joe wants to get married.
CAROLINE	Married! Before you finish your education? That's ridiculous. You're too young to get married, anyway. Diana, oh, Diana, all the plans, all the work. What a waste.
DIANA	A waste! Is that what you think? Sometimes your perfect little world gets upset. Sometimes you can't plan. Sometimes you only have time to react. And, to tell someone. To tell someone who cares about you that you need their help, their advice.
CAROLINE	I just can't see what we, ...can do. I'm so disappointed.
DIANA	Well, that's not news, at least. Maybe if we had been smarter, used condoms, or if you had let me go on the pill last spring when I asked. But that was one plan you never liked..
CAROLINE	I can't see what the next step is; where we go from here. What about your career?
DIANA	Plans? This is not about plans, Mom. This is about me. And Joe. And the baby. If you can't handle that, then I can't handle you. Here's the money for the lunch. Next time, it's on you. (*she rises to leave*)
CAROLINE	Diana, I..

DIANA exits. Her mother follows her with her eyes, then lowers her head in her hands.

* * *

Scene 6

from "Video Wars"

by Rex Deverell

3 or 4 characters

HANGIN' AT THE HANDY

    Rex Deverell is widely known in Canadian theatre as the writer of award-winning plays such as "Boiler Room Suite", and as playwright-in-residence at the Globe Theatre in Regina (1975-1990). He also has been published in a great book of plays for youth called, *Plays of Belonging*, from which comes this excerpt from "Video Wars".

    Nick and his gang are all about fourteen. They hang out at the corner store after school, which is run by Kim, around the same age, and his family. Billie and Darin look up to Nick and generally follow his lead. In "Video Wars", Nick, Kim and Darin are male, and Billie is female, but any combination of gender can have fun with this quick, comic scene. You can also combine Kim and Darin to create a script for only three actors if you wish.

    This is the opening scene of the play. Nick manages the scene by using **direct address**, (a technique described earlier in the introduction to the VICTOR AND ROCKY scene). As in *Act I, Scene 1* of "Romeo and Juliet", Rex Deverell knows that fast-paced, exciting openings are what audiences like to watch, so be prepared to use all of the stage area during this scene, just as you would in a good sword-fight, and know all the **exit and entrance cues**, so it looks good. You also have to be younger, then older, then a character your own age — in other words, you have to play more than one role. Actors call this **doubling**. Make these characters easy to recognize, and comic, and keep your **line cues** quick. Whew, that's a lot of work.

Hangin' at the Handy

	The interior of The Handy Corner Store, a small neighbourhood variety shop. The owners have recently installed an electronic video game to see if it will improve business. The store is near a school and from time to time the sounds of the school yard can be heard through the walls of the store. NICK enters wearing the latest cocky flamboyant style. He addresses the audience.
NICK	Hi. I want to tell you about something that happened to me — oh, my name's Nick — anyway, something kinda important that happened to me one afternoon. I'll set the scene for you. This is THE HANDY DANDY CORNER GROCERY STORE — "The Handy" for short.
	In the distance there is the sound of a school bell and children pouring into the playground.
	That's the school I go to — right across the road. Me and my friends come in here all the time. You know before school, bubble gum; at noon, Orange Sloshy Slurpies and stuff; after school, Chocolate Barfies and Bitter Sour Lemon twists — if we've got any money left. Kids come in here in like waves. First the little kids.
	Suddenly the stage seems full of youngsters running around the store. They come up to the counter and address an unseen storekeeper.
DARIN	I want a cream soda!

Two for the Show / 29

BILLIE　　I want a Sloshy Slurpy. A little one. No, a big one. One with Smarties in it.

KIM　　I want a red licorice. Is this enough money?

DARIN　　*(to NICK)* Gimme a dime, okay? Okay? Gimme a dime! That's all I need to get some pop, okay? Gimme a dime.

BILLIE　　Don't put those kind of Smarties. I just want the red ones. I said the red ones. I don't want those green kind. Take them out! Take them out! Yechhh!

KIM　　How many can I have for this much money?

DARIN　　Just give me a nickel, okay? Please? Pretty please. Aw, c'mon! One little nickel?

NICK　　Out!

They vanish and the stage is quiet again.

NICK　　Those were the little kids. Then a bunch of Senior High kids come in...

The actors return as teenagers — the unimpressionable age.

KIM　　I'm cool.

BILLIE　　I'm cool.

DARIN　　I'm very cool.

KIM　　A tube of Clearasil, please.

DARIN　　What are you doing tonight?

BILLIE　　I don't know. Maybe I'll call Stephie — unless Allison calls me in which case I'll call you but I probably won't because Dan called yesterday and he said that Laurie and Melanie were over and — you know. Or

	maybe I'll wash my hair. What are you doing tonight?
KIM	I don't know. Nothing, I guess — life is so boring.
DARIN	Yeah, boring.
BILLIE	Yeah. Call me, okay?
KIM	Okay.
BILLIE	Okay?
DARIN	Okay.
BILLIE	Okay.
	The teenagers begin to leave.
KIM	Am I getting a zit right here? Do you see a zit?
	Exit.
NICK	Those were the big kids. (*calling after them*) Get a life why doncha? (*to the audience*) And after that we take over — me and kids in my class.
	DARIN and BILLIE return in their roles as NICK's classmates, sauntering through the store like gangsters — clearly in charge.
DARIN	Yo, Nick!
NICK	Yo, Darin! (*to audience*) That's Darin.
DARIN	Say what, Dude!
NICK	What!
	They break up.

BILLIE	Yo, Guys.
NICK & DARIN	Yo, Billie!
NICK	*(to audience)* This is Billie.
BILLIE	Give me "five"!
NICK & DARIN	Five!
NICK	*(aside to audience)* Us. The only kids that matter.

DARIN and BILLIE strike poses with NICK

* * *

Scene 7

from "The Body Image Project"

by Eleanor Albanese

2 females / 1 male

QUINN'S ADVICE

This scene is about Mari's relationship with David, someone her girlfriend, Quinn, thinks is wrong for Mari. Check the earlier introduction to Scene 3, or read that scene for more details. This scene happens a few days later at school.

One of the most tense moments in this scene is the **beat** between David's entrance and Quinn's exit. Quinn barely acknowledges David, and vice versa, and the audience should see that they can't stand one another. Since they don't share any dialogue, how can't both actors show their feelings? Don't go overboard — audiences can see even the quickest of **gestures** or **reactions** if they are well-timed and 'given their moment.'

Like the last scene, this scene also calls for a school bell to ring. Put the sound on tape and get someone to be your **sound tech**. so that it rings at the right moment.

QUINN'S ADVICE

MARI is sitting by herself. QUINN enters carrying a brown paper bag. She throws the bag in front of MARI.

QUINN   Tah-dah.

MARI   What's this?

QUINN   Muffins. And you better eat them because I slaved in my mother's kitchen for over an hour making them last night.

MARI   Why's everyone trying to make me eat?

QUINN   Sorry. It's just that I was eating breakfast yesterday, reading the cereal box, so I wouldn't have to listen to my annoying brother. Anyway, I see this recipe for Low-Cal muffins. And my brain went — Mari! You know, since you're so worried about every iddy-biddy calorie.

MARI   Look who's talking. You're the one who started smoking just to lose weight.

QUINN   That's different.

MARI   Oh right, you'll just die of cancer, that's all.

QUINN   At least I won't be obsessing every minute of my life about calories. Next thing, you'll be telling me there's calories in the air.

MARI   No. But I'll have you know that there are calories in non-foods.

QUINN   Non-foods? You mean, as in beds and cars and stuff like that?

MARI   No. As in mouthwash and toothpaste.

QUINN   Oh Mari. Thank you for saving my life. I was going to have a bowl of toothpaste for lunch, but instead I'll have some low-cal mouthwash.

            MARI laughs.

QUINN   Do you want to try a muffin or do you need to dissect it in Mr. Suzack's lab class first?

MARI   Wasn't that gross yesterday — with the frogs? And then when Cindy kept asking him what sex they were, I thought I was going to choke.

QUINN   I think Cindy watches too many soap operas. Her brain is seriously warped. So... (*taking a muffin out of the bag, in a spooky voice*) are you ready to try one?

MARI   I will. Just ... later.

QUINN   Why are you so strict on this diet anyway?

MARI   I have to be strict because my mother forces me to eat her food. She cooks like she's back in the old country — like we're farmers or something.

QUINN   At least she cooks. We have to nuke frozen dinners every night.

MARI   I know. I'm just saying—

QUINN   Forget it. Forget it. What I really want to know is what's going on with you and David?

MARI   Nothing.

QUINN   Nothing.

MARI	Oh, except my mom found out about him, so I've got to be really careful now.
QUINN	How'd she find out?
MARI	He sent flowers.
QUINN	What a jerk.
MARI	No one's ever sent me flowers before. They were beautiful.
QUINN	But he knows how strict your parents are. So what are you going to do now?
MARI	I don't know. Everything's gone crazy.
QUINN	Like how?
MARI	David and I seem to be fighting all the time. Quinn, what am I doing wrong?
QUINN	Try 'nothing'.
MARI	But I keep screwing things up, I know I do. I never want to be alone with him. The guy must think I'm so weird.
QUINN	I wouldn't want to be alone with a guy who was pressuring me. I've seen the way he is with you.
MARI	He's not like that all the time.
	DAVID enters. He sits beside MARI, putting his arm around her.
DAVID	Hi.
QUINN	I gotta go. Hey Mari, why don't you come bowling with us after school?
DAVID	Bowling? Ah, you're joking, right?

QUINN (*ignoring DAVID's comment and talking only to MARI*) It's really cool. You get to wear these funky shoes. And there's all these bald guys with their wives. We killed ourselves laughing last time.

MARI I used to like bowling.

QUINN Then come! You could come too David. I mean, you guys don't have to be alone every single minute.

DAVID We've got plans. Maybe some other time.

School bell rings.

QUINN Whatever. See ya Mari, in Suzack's class, eh?

MARI Hope it's as good as yesterday. (*giggling*)

QUINN exits. MARI starts to go.

DAVID Sit down.

MARI I'll be late for class.

DAVID What are you telling her?

MARI Who Quinn? Nothing.

DAVID What's going on Mari?

MARI I don't know what you mean.

DAVID You sure had enough to say to your little friend a few minutes ago. (*imitating MARI's voice*) "Hope it's as good as yesterday". You got a crush on Suzack or something?

MARI David, I don't know what you're talking about.

DAVID   You don't know what I'm talking about. I'm sick of your little innocent act, you know that.

MARI   What act? Everything I tell you is true.

DAVID   Yeah right. You wouldn't know the truth if it hit you in the face.

MARI   Why do you say stuff like that?

DAVID   Go back to your Mommy and Daddy, why don't you. Talk to me in five years when you grow up.

>   *DAVID exits. MARI is left alone, and very upset.*

* * *

Scene 8

from "Yellow on Thursdays"

by Sara Graefe

2 females / 1 male

KATIE

    This is the first of two scenes taken from Sara Graefe's short play about adolescent sexuality. Rebecca and Katie are best friends; Mike is a new guy in class, from Montreal, and as you can read, Rebecca wastes no time getting to know him better.

    Although the Rebecca and Mike are the key event of the scene, Katie is the main character in the play. In this scene, Katie must stand by and watch as her best friend gets a new 'best' friend. Notice that during the **beat** when Rebecca asks Mike for a date, Katie says very little but must stand there listening. Don't just stand there. Many times on stage, it is how a character reacts to new circumstances that tells the audience all about her. As a matter of fact, how could you stage this scene so that the action between Mike and Rebecca is seen by the audience as *less* important than Katie's reaction? In other words, force the audience to **focus** on the character who is *not* speaking?

    Sara Graefe started writing when she was at Gloucester High School in Ottawa. By the time she graduated, she had won the National Arts Centre's Young Playwright's Search a total of three times.

KATIE

>*KATIE and MIKE in French class. She stares dreamily at the teacher.*

MIKE　　Hey.

>*KATIE stares. He waves at her. She looks like she's been caught with her hand in the cookie jar. She busies her self with her notes.*

MIKE　　Hey, you! Cathy or whatever.

KATIE　　Katie.

MIKE　　Katie. You look real familiar. I mean, I think I saw you in the hall yesterday, right?

KATIE　　Yeah.

>*They stare at one another intensely. The bell rings. She hurries out, overwhelmed.*

MIKE　　Hey wait—

>*KATIE runs into REBECCA in the hall.*

REBECCA　　Hey, what's with you?

KATIE　　It's just too much.

REBECCA　　What?

KATIE　　French class.

>*MIKE appears in the hall.*

REBECCA　　He's in your class?

KATIE　　Sits right next to me. Alphabetical order.

REBECCA   Well, no wonder... Hey there, Mike!

MIKE   Hey, Rebecca. Katie.

                He keeps walking.

REBECCA   Hey, Mike, wait up!

KATIE   Yeah, no wonder, alright...

                REBECCA catches up to MIKE, KATIE in tow.

MIKE   So how's it going?

REBECCA   Good. You?

MIKE   OK.

REBECCA   Surviving so far?

MIKE   Oh yeah, no sweat.

REBECCA   Although I'm sure it's BLAHSville after (*a bad French accent*) Mont-ray-al.

MIKE   Hey, could be worse, eh? At least the people here are nice.

REBECCA   You think? That's good. We like to make people feel right at home, don't we Katie? Katie?

KATIE   Sure.

REBECCA   So...

MIKE   So...

                They laugh.

REBECCA   What are you up to tonight?

MIKE   Not much...

REBECCA   Would you like to come over or something?

MIKE   Or something?!

REBECCA   Just whatever. We could watch "The Simpsons", hang out, y'know... Your very own personal Welcome Wagon!

MIKE   Sounds good.

REBECCA   Plus my parents are going to be out so we'll have the whole place to ourselves.

MIKE   Hey, great.

REBECCA   How about you come by 'round seven? Here... (*grabbing his binder and scribbling on it*) 5375 Windsor. Right near 41st and Fraser, OK?

MIKE   Yeah, I can figure it out.

REBECCA   Great — so see you then?

MIKE   Yeah, see you then.

MIKE leaves, making a "right on" sign to himself. REBECCA stares after him.

REBECCA   I can't believe I just did that. I can't believe he said yes. Isn't this amazing?

KATIE   I thought we were going to the movies tonight.

REBECCA   Oh shoot. I completely forgot! We'll go next Tuesday instead, I promise, swear-to-God— I mean, Katie, the opportunity was just sitting there right in front of my nose, how could I not take it? Especially with my parents out and my sister at night class. It's like it's meant to be, right? I may never get another chance like this again. You understand, don't you, Katie?

KATIE   Yeah, whatever.

REBECCA   Oh, come on — Saliva Sisters, right? You know I'd do the same for you in this situation.

KATIE   But I've never— Never mind.

REBECCA   You mad?

KATIE   No.

REBECCA   You are, kinda.

KATIE   Look, it's OK.

REBECCA   Katie...

KATIE   Let's just drop it.

REBECCA   I promise to tell you all about it. All the juicy details. OK?

KATIE   OK.

REBECCA makes her Saliva Sisters sign. KATIE manages a smile.

KATIE   Oh, you lucky thing, you!

REBECCA
& KATIE   MIKE WILLIAMS!!!

They squeal.

* * *

Scene 9

from "Weird Kid"

by Rex Deverell

2 females / 2 males

JENNIFER'S STORY

The 'weird kid' in this scene, Babs, has successfully got revenge on her tormentors, Ben, Tim, Trish and Jennifer, by trashing a room at school, and leaving evidence that points to them. As a result, the four kids are forced to clean up the mess that Babs created.

As the four start to recreate their individual encounters with Babs, (through a mock trial scene staged by Ben) they begin to understand Babs more and realize that they have misjudged her — she's not 'weird', just different from them.

Babs is not in this scene, so Ben has to 'play' her in the scene with Jennifer and Trish, who play themselves in the past. But, since Tim has only a few lines, he could play 'Babs' instead and leave the Ben as 'the lawyer." Tim as Babs could have a *little* fun to start as a guy trying to act like a girl, but don't forget the main point of the scene is to understand Babs' true feelings; feeling left out is an emotion we've all experienced.

This type of scene is called **a play within a play**, and is a common device for playwrights. Actors and audience enjoy it because it allows one actor to play two roles in the same play.

Jennifer's Story

> *A high school classroom. BEN, TIM, JENNIFER, and TRISH clean up an obvious mess — papers all over, desks overturned, etc. BEN poses as a criminal lawyer. The 'judge' can be played by Tim or be an imaginary character.*

BEN — Well, Your Honour — we admit that we looked down on the defendant. We admit we judged her. In fact it's getting to look more and more like she's the only one who had enough reasons to want to get us into deeper - difficulty, Sir.

TRISH — That's right.

TIM — Okay. What else have we got? Jen, what about the time—

JENNIFER — Isn't this enough? *(starting for the door)* Hey, Ben, that sounds good, eh? Let's go.

TIM — What's your hurry?

JENNIFER — Let's get it over with.

TIM — What about the time you were best friends with her?

JENNIFER — It didn't last very long.

BEN — Yeah — what was that about, anyway?

JENNIFER — Nothing.

TIM — Well, tell us then.

JENNIFER — It's my business.

TRISH   What is?

JENNIFER   It's not something I'm proud of, okay?

             Pause.

JENNIFER   Alright, you know how last year I was new at this school — and it took a long time to make friends with anybody and finally you guys got to be my friends. Well for a while this year Trish started to act kinda strange —

TRISH   I did not!

JENNIFER   I mean you were going to movies and stuff with Ben and Tim — and you wouldn't call me up or anything and see if I might want to go, you know what I mean?

TRISH   *(surprised)* Really?

JENNIFER   Yes, really. So I kinda made up with Babs.

TRISH   What a choice.

JENNIFER   To get back at you.

TRISH   Oh. But I didn't do that on purpose.

JENNIFER   I know that now—

TRISH   Oh, Jen...

JENNIFER   Oh, Trish...

             The boys are about to vomit.

TIM   I hate to break in on this intimate scene — but we're talking about Babs.

JENNIFER   Yeah, Babs. Well, she just got caught in the middle. I guess the worse part of it was when I made arrangements to go shopping with her.

TRISH	The day I ran into you at Market Square Mall?
JENNIFER	I kinda planned that too. I knew you'd probably show up. *(to BEN)* You be Babs this time.
BEN	Yucky girls' stuff. Let Trish do it. She hasn't done it yet—
JENNIFER	No, Trish is in this.
BEN	*(resigned)* What do I do?
JENNIFER	Well, it took me a while to persuade her to come. She said she didn't want to buy anything and she didn't have the money to take the bus downtown — and I said come on anyway because I'd gotten a lot of money for my birthday from my grandmother and I still need to buy a pair of jeans or something and *(to BEN)* you have such great taste...
TRISH	Oh boy.
JENNIFER	Right. Anyway that's what I told her and *(to BEN)* you fall for it and my mom gives us a ride and drops us off ... but you still don't have any money... What are you going to get, Babs?
BEN	*(playing the part realistically)* I told you I couldn't buy anything.
JENNIFER	*(keeping an eye out for TRISH)* I know — but I thought you probably could buy some little thing.
BEN	Well, I can't. Let's go and get your— boy, look at that.
JENNIFER	What?

BEN	That dirt bike — no, she wouldn't be interested in a dirt bike
JENNIFER	It was one of those keyboard things — electronic piano or something. How did you know she stopped like that?
BEN	If she's like me — whenever I don't have any money I always see something really expensive I'd really like. That really bugs me.
JENNIFER	She looked at it like she'd never be able to buy it — not in a thousand years.
BEN	(as Babs) Those keyboards — you can make any sound you could ever want. You don't even have to write it down or anything. You just play it and it plays back what ever you think up.
JENNIFER	It's probably not that easy, Babs. Let's start with Chez Lean Jeans — and if they don't have anything maybe Jiffy Sports and then I'll try Eatons and maybe Zellers, okay? Hey, look at those...
BEN	They're nice...
JENNIFER	No — they're too ordinary...
BEN	Are you sure you want me to help?
JENNIFER	I wouldn't have asked you, would I?
BEN	I guess not...
JENNIFER	(suddenly) There's Trish Klein. (waving) Hi, Trish.
TRISH	(coming over) Hi, Jenny. Fancy meeting you.
JENNIFER	Say hello to my very good friend, Babs.

TRISH	Hello, Babs.
BEN	Hullo.
TRISH	So what are you doing?
JENNIFER	Buying some jeans. Babs is helping me, aren't you, Babs?
BEN	I guess so.
TRISH	How come I haven't heard from you?
JENNIFER	How come I haven't heard from *you*?
TRISH	I thought you'd call.
JENNIFER	I thought *you'd* call.

Pause.

TRISH	Are you going to the party tonight?
JENNIFER	What party?
TRISH	Ben and Tim are cooking something up. They said they were inviting you.
JENNIFER	I don't know...
TRISH	You can come. Hey, I'll stop on the way and we can walk over together, okay?
JENNIFER	I'll think about it. I'll probably come. Yeah, I'll come. What time?
TRISH	Eight.
JENNIFER	Great!
TRISH	What sort of jeans are you going to buy?
JENNIFER	I don't know. Got any ideas?

TRISH	To tell you the truth there's this new brand over at the Slack Shack? I've been thinking about — you know — at least trying on a pair. Wanna go over there?
JENNIFER	Sure! *(to Babs as an after thought)* Coming?
BEN	No, it's alright. Go ahead.
JENNIFER	*(breaking out of the scene)* That's exactly the way she sounded. You could have been there. How did you know?
BEN	I sorta guessed.
TIM	There's a picture coming clear.
BEN	And so, your Honour, Sir, perhaps you can see a history of meanness, a building up of hurt and little insults, a powder keg, as they say, just waiting to explode.
JENNIFER	Yeah.

* * *

Scene 10

from "That's No Lady, That's My Immigrant!"

by Sandra Dempsey

1 female / 1 male

BARBIE AND KEN

 This is a very funny scene. Sandra Dempsey, writer of numerous award-winning plays, has taken everyone's favourite dolls, Barbie and Ken, and given them a baby. But Barbie has another little surprise for Ken ....

 Keeping your **concentration** and staying in character are essential for the humour in the scene. It also requires **physical comedy** — both Barbie and Ken "move and speak in a plastic manner," as Sandra Dempsey says in her stage directions. Try walking and talking like dolls before memorizing this one. Then add the **lines**, the **timing** and Ken's **over-reaction** to the news. If you can get Barbie and Ken-like **costumes** and a real Kamper, the audience would love it even more. What would Barbie's hospital room look like anyway...?

Playwright's note: Barbie and Ken are anatomically incorrect Caucasian dolls manufactured in China.

Barbie and Ken

>BARBIE's *room on the maternity ward. She is lying in bed, having just returned from giving birth. KEN comes to visit her for the first time since the big event. He's carrying a shopping bag. Both characters move and speak in a 'plastic' manner.*

KEN (*bursts into the room*) Barbie!

BARBIE Ken.

KEN (*he sits beside her bed*) I would have been here sooner but it took a long time to find a safe spot to park my Ken-Kar-with retractable-roof-and-honk-a-horn-that-really-works!

BARBIE I know you love your Ken-Kar, Ken.

KEN I'll say! Boy — best thing we ever did was trade in that old Barbie-Beach-buggie.

BARBIE So you keep telling me.

KEN Besides, I fit better behind the wheel.

BARBIE You're not the *only* one who fits, Ken.

KEN Now dear, I can drive you everywhere.

BARBIE I know, Ken. You even drive me up the wall.

KEN I don't mind, honest. So long as I'm not busy changing outfits.

BARBIE Of course.

KEN The nurse said I could only stay a few minutes. Gosh but I've missed you. Our neighbours have missed you. There are piles of dishes and washing and ironing waiting for you to come home too!

And I've been telling everybody about our little Midge.

BARBIE I can tell you're a proud Papa already.

KEN I'm proud of my Barbie, that's for sure. (*he reaches into the shopping bag and pulls items out*) Here, I brought you some new hair!

And, some Malibu pills. And, best of all, guess what I bought today!?

BARBIE I don't know, Ken.

KEN Come on. Just take a guess.

BARBIE (*angry*) Ken, I've just delivered a doll. I'm tired and besides...

KEN (*cutting her off*) Okay, honey. Are you ready for this? I bought a Barbie & Ken Kamper! We'll be able to get away and experience nature — just the three of us: you, me, and... Say, where is my little Midge anyway?

BARBIE She's resting in her box, Ken...

KEN Golly, won't it be fun when she sees Pretty Pony Palomino.

BARBIE And more fun when she gets to muck out all those Pretty Pony Palomino road apples.

KEN Jeepers. I hope I get to see her soon. I've been handing out chocolate cigars to everyone I meet — I'm just about out of stock!

BARBIE Ken, I think there's something I should discuss with you before we go any further...

KEN	What is it, my Bendable Barbie? You look worried.
BARBIE	It's about Midge.
KEN	What about our little Midget?
BARBIE	Now, Ken, I don't want you to get upset. You know if you get so much as a slight temperature, you start to melt.
KEN	I know, I know. Now what about Midge?
BARBIE	Promise you won't get mad?
KEN	Promise. Now tell me.
BARBIE	(*very hesitatingly*) Well, she's *different*, that's all.
KEN	Different? What do you mean she's different? What's wrong with her!?
BARBIE	Nothing's *wrong* with her. It's just ... well...
KEN	Barbie, we've never had any secrets between us. Now out with it.
BARBIE	Well...
KEN	I'm going to start dripping in a minute!
BARBIE	(*finally blurting it out*) She's made in Japan!
KEN	Oh Mattel! How could this happen!?
BARBIE	There's nothing wrong with her. She was just imported, that's all.
KEN	It was him, wasn't it!? It was that G.I. Joe, wasn't it!??
BARBIE	No, Ken it wasn't. You're just making that up.

KEN "Fighting man from head to toe' — my foot! (*repacking the shopping bag*) Well that's it — I'm returning the Kamper — and the special Barbie Fashion Boutique; that was going to be your surprise — not any more, boy!!

BARBIE Oh, Ken. Don't be angry. Remember your passive-aggressive stress-management exercises.

KEN snaps a cigar and holds onto the butt.

KEN Ha! No wonder you wanted me to sign up for all those classes! I bet *that's* when you were busy entertaining the troops.

BARBIE That's not true! Midge belongs to us!

KEN To you! Not to us! I'm not having anything to do with her!

BARBIE Ken! How can you say that?

KEN No doll of mine comes from Japan! If I'm going to have a doll, she's going to be just like me! Not one of those ... those .... yuck, I fell sick just thinking about it!

BARBIE Ken, control yourself. Why don't you go have a pretend cup of coffee and try to cool down a bit?

KEN There's nothing to cool down about! She's made in Japan and that's that! Oh, Hasbro. I need a pretend whiskey!

BARBIE Oh, just go have a time-out and light up your butt. You'll feel differently in the morning, I know you will.

KEN (*tossing the cigar butt into the bag*) No I won't! G.I. Joe — oh this is sick!
To think, I was going to get my plastic hair re-painted Barbie Blond just for you!

|||(*jumping up to leave*) I'm getting out of here. That's it, Barbie! That's the last straw! We're finished! I'm moving out! And that little mutant Midget won't get a plastic penny out of my seersucker polyester Ken Pants either!

BARBIE | But where will you go?

KEN | (*he has to think for a minute*) Tonka Toys'll take me — I'll go there. Oh this is sick!

He storms out.

BARBIE | Oh, ever since our Skipper ran off with that Kommander Karl Kung-Fu doll, he just hasn't been the same.

* * *

Section Two — TWO FOR THE SHOW

Now that direct address, a play within a play, doubling, using words from another language, comic stereotypes, acting a transition, playing someone older or younger — and other techniques that make acting enjoyable — are skills in your repertoire, the scenes in this section should be a challenge.

The scenes listed below all employ one or more of the techniques introduced in Section One as a *key* element of the scene. Three scenes in this group are written by another excellent Canadian playwright you should know about, Dennis Foon. He has published four plays in two different books called *New Canadian Kid/ Invisible Kid* (Pulp, Vancouver, 1989) and *Skin and Liars* (Playwrights Canada Press, Toronto, 1988) that are perfect pieces to try if you like the short excerpts provided here. There is also a comic scene by Carol Shields that will have you laughing, another comic, but tender, moment about a mail-order bride by Rick Salutin, and two scenes from "Thin Ice" that are about what girls talk about when guys aren't around, and what guys talk about ... ahh, you know the rest.

Most of these scenes are just a little bit longer as well — so make sure you spend the extra time during line rehearsal. And break two legs, OK?

Scene 11

from "Skin"

by Dennis Foon

1 female / 1 male or female

MR. LIZARD

Dennis Foon is arguably Canada's best known writer and director of theatre for young audiences. He co-founded Green Thumb Theatre of Vancouver and has won numerous national and international awards for playwrighting, screenplays and radio drama. This scene is from his one-act play, "Skin".

MR. LIZARD is a great opportunity for **doubling.** The actor who plays Delacy, should also play the inimitable Mr. Lizard, Jennifer's *least* favourite teacher. Mr. Lizard should be played with a mask. One of those ugly, rubber, dinosaur, Hallowe'en masks would be perfect, or construct a simple, but scary mask using felt pens and half a paper bag. Don't forget that it is his lizard-like movements and voice that really bring Jennifer's nemesis to life.

At the stage direction 'Mr. Lizard exits', think of an interesting **transition** that can transform Mr. Lizard to Delacy in one graceful movement (or light change) without anyone really leaving the stage.

MR. LIZARD

JENNIFER	Like I said, school was really a cinch. All my teachers were really nice too. Except for one — Mr. Lizard.
	MR. LIZARD slowly enters, his green clawed hands emerging first. He wears a sports jacket and tie and has a very green lizard mask. He sees a fly, swats it out of the air and eats it with gusto.
MR. LIZARD	Passing notes again, Miss Malcolm?
JENNIFER	No, Mr. Lizard.
MR. LIZARD	I saw You passing notes, Miss Malcolm.
JENNIFER	But sir—
MR. LIZARD	No buts. Out. You. Go.
JENNIFER	Or he'd—
MR. LIZARD	What was so funny about that, Miss Malcolm?
JENNIFER	Nothing, Mr. Lizard.
MR. LIZARD	Then why were you laughing?
JENNIFER	I wasn't laughing, sir.
MR. LIZARD	Then what did I hear?
JENNIFER	I don't know, sir,
MR. LIZARD	Out. You. Go.
JENNIFER	Mr. Lizard always singled me out, I didn't know why. He considered me a loser.

MR. LIZARD	You, Miss Malcolm, have an atrocious attitude toward the learning process.
JENNIFER	I do?
MR. LIZARD	You are lazy. You don't have what it takes.
JENNIFER	That's not fair.
MR. LIZARD	It's an objective assessment.
JENNIFER	No it's not.
MR. LIZARD	Are you being smart with me, young lady?
JENNIFER	Yes, that's exactly what I am, smart. I'm a lot smarter than you think.
MR. LIZARD	Out. You. Go.
	MR. LIZARD exits.
DELACY	You know, he did the same thing to me when I was in his class.
JENNIFER	Really, Delacy?
DELACY	The old Lizard of Oz used to pick on me all the time too.
JENNIFER	He did?
DELACY	All he figured I was good for was athletics. Come to think of it, a lot of my teachers thought I was definite sports material.
JENNIFER	You? Why?
DELACY	Beats me. Funny, though, nobody ever encouraged me to be a scientist. Anybody ever encourage you?
JENNIFER	No.

DELACY	Come to think of it-why are you in vocational school?
JENNIFER	Because my counsellor thought it was a good idea.
DELACY	If your counsellor thought it was a good idea, would you jump in a lake?
JENNIFER	Not if it was Lake Erie.
DELACY	You're smart-smart enough to go to university. Why aren't you in a collegiate?
JENNIFER	Cause I'm lazy.
DELACY	That's what Mr. Lizard says. But I've seen how hard you can work when you're interested in something. You're not lazy.
JENNIFER	I am at school.
DELACY	Maybe they're boring you. If you tried, you could go to university. You should.
JENNIFER	No way. *(to audience)* But I wondered about that. Why was I doing what I was doing? I never knew if I was smart or not because I never really tried ... but what if I did? Why not? I had nothing to lose.

***

Scene 12

from "Thin Ice"

by Beverley Cooper & Banuta Rubess

2 females / 1 or 2 males

FANTASY DATE

    This scene is the first of two scenes taken from "Thin Ice", an hard-hitting and humourous one-act play about Trish, Jennifer, Des and Tony and teenage sexual relations. Here, the two girls make a angry prank phone call to Ron (Tony's brother) after hearing that, on a date, he hit his girlfriend, Sally. Then, they fantasize about how the 'perfect date' would act.

    In the play, Tony and Des both appear in the **dream sequence**, because they are both on another part of the stage at the same time, but *one* male actor can easily **double** for our purposes, playing the rich, charmer and then the rough bad boy (the two lines of dialogue after Tony's exit give just enough time to exit and re-enter, **transformed** as Des, the bad boy.) Well-timed light changes would emphasize the dream sequences, and perhaps, using different colour **gels**, even underscore the contrast between the two fantasies.

    "Thin Ice" won a prestigious Dora Mavor Moore Award for both its authors in 1987. Since then, both Banuta Rubess, who writes and directs, and Beverley Cooper, who writes and acts, have had continuing success on radio, in print and on stages across Canada.

Fantasy Date

JENNIFER   (*laughing*) Trish, no. You wouldn't dare.

TRISH   (*looking through the telephone book*) Oh yeah?

JENNIFER   (*hiding her face*) I don't believe you.

> TRISH dials.

TRISH   (*after dialing*) Shhh! It's ringing. (*disguising voice*) Hello Ron? You don't know me but I know you ... I know what you did — to Sally, you sicko! And don't think I won't report you to the cops, 'cos I will, jerk—

> Angry squawking comes out of the phone. JENNIFER grabs the phone and joins in.

JENNIFER   (*disguising voice*) We know where you are and we're coming over to get you right now.

> JENNIFER hangs up and she explodes into laughter.

TRISH   Jennifer! It's not funny you know. Sally's been really weird ever since. She never goes out. She's always crying. And I hear she's quitting school.

JENNIFER   Wow. I can't believe Ron would do something like that.

TRISH   Believe it.

JENNIFER   Besides it's not rape if you know the guy.

TRISH   What is it then? A love tap?! Don't be so naive. If a girl doesn't want to do it and the guy makes her, it's rape.

JENNIFER	Alright. You don't need to yell.
TRISH	Well it just makes me so mad when people insinuate that the girl is asking for it. No one asks for it.
JENNIFER	Well I know what to do ... I saw on TV how, like, you hold your keys like this and if someone jumps you from behind you put your finger in his eye and stuff.
TRISH	Jennifer! What are you going to do, walk around the party with brass knuckles?
JENNIFER	They're two separate people, Ron and Tony, you know, they're not Siamese twins. I'd be more worried about Des. Still waters run deep you know.
TRISH	What? He's in Grade 12. He's not Rambo, he's a guy who's smart and plays hockey ... he's normal. Anyway, it's just a party. I suppose your idea of a good time is for some prince to say Rapunzel, Rapunzel, let down your hair or something.
JENNIFER	It is not. It's...
	Corny music. The scene changes into perfect date fantasy — bing bong, the door bell rings.
JENNIFER	I'll get it. (*opens the door for TONY who is dressed in a tuxedo*) Hi, Tony.
TONY	Hello, Jennifer, you look very pretty tonight. This is for you.
	TONY hands JENNIFER a flower.
JENNIFER	Why...thank you, Tony, it's beautiful. Come on in.
TONY	I've got a surprise for you.

JENNIFER   Really?

TONY   I've got a white limousine waiting. We're going to take one of my jets and spend the evening in Rio de Janeiro.

JENNIFER   Are you crazy?

TONY   No, just rich. I just won 14 million dollars in a lottery.

JENNIFER   I better get changed.

TONY   I've already bought you ten new designer outfits.

JENNIFER   I don't know if my parents will go for it.

TONY   Your parents think it's fine, I've already talked to them.

TONY takes JENNIFER's hand and leads her away.

JENNIFER   What about school?

TONY   You don't have to go to school. I finished it for you.

TONY exits.

JENNIFER   And then we jet around the world in his purple private plane.

TRISH   That sounds like the most boring event since my last visit to the dentist. To me the perfect evening is more intimate. More dangerous.

Scene change to TRISH's fantasy. TRISH is fixing her hair when DES bursts in.

TRISH   Don't you ever knock?

DES	I had to see you. I couldn't wait.
	DES takes TRISH in his arms, but she pushes him away.
TRISH	Don't you manhandle me.
DES	I couldn't help myself. I've been dreaming about you all day.
TRISH	Well just keep your cool for a few minutes while I get ready.
DES	You look gorgeous, that dress is very sexy ... and what's that perfume you're wearing? Not Poison? You know how it drives me wild...
TRISH	(*laughing*) Oh Des ... you animal.
DES	C'mere baby. (*grabbing her roughly*)
TRISH	Hey.
DES	Just like on TV.
	DES pulls TRISH roughly.
TRISH	Owww. (*pushing DES away, as he exits*) That hurt! They never get bruises on *Melrose Place*.

* * *

Scene 13

"Robbie's Secret"

by Brian Kennedy

2 males

In this scene I've attempted to give the actors a little character 'meat' to chew on.

These two petty thieves could be from any era, in any major city - I pictured the 1950's in Toronto, and if the actors dress in old suits and fedoras this would be a perfect effect.

If you decide not to use costume to help show character, you will have to **physicalize.** This means Robbie's age — and his bad leg — and Doug's large body slowness will have to be front and centre. There are some fairly specific emotional directions for each character as well.

I like to think that the siren at the first and the last moments, round out the scene, so get yourselves a **sound tech.** and rehearse the cues before performance.

Don't forget — these two characters are not like you and your partner - they're bigger, older, and far more street-wise. If that isn't enough, the cops could bust in at any moment. And, like all criminals, deep down, they're scared. This is not a comedy - to them.

Robbie's Secret

Robbie, 60, a lifetime criminal, but likable loser; nervous.

Doug late 20's, slow-moving, his partner in crime.

In The Pizza Palace, a rundown restaurant. It is 2 a.m. Sound of a police siren outside. ROBBIE enters first, and quickly sits at a table. In spite of his age — looks like a kid who has finally reached home safely.

ROBBIE   (*to a waiter, off-stage*) Coffee ... No, two. Better make that two coffee.

He nervously rubs his hands together. DOUG enters cool and slow, the opposite of ROBBIE's rushed entrance.

ROBBIE   Hey, Doug. Over here.

DOUG   Yeah, (*mimics ROBBIE's nervous voice*) 'Over here'. I can see that, ya goof. There's a distinct lack of customers this time in the morning. (*threatening*) Just the way I like it.

ROBBIE   Listen, Doug, I...

DOUG   ... screwed up. Again.

ROBBIE   No, Dougie, you got to believe me, I was just standing there, like you told me too, my leg was killing me like usual and this cruiser came round the corner. They were gonna see me for sure. They had their flashlights covering the alley, their high beams on the street. I had to move fast or we both woulda been cooked.

DOUG   Leaving me with the goods and a big surprise. I oughta level you right here (*raising hand, then lowering it*). Ahh, it ain't worth it. You're just too much of a loser already, Robbie. It would be too easy. Besides, I'd hate to leave a mess this late for the waiter. Where is that son of a... (*shouts*) Andy!

Ah, I guess I'll have to get it myself...

ROBBIE   Here, let me do it, let me. And, thanks, Dougie. Thanks. I won't forget this.

DOUG   That's what I'm afraid of.

ROBBIE   Here you go, Doug. Sugar?

DOUG   Robbie, you're getting too old for this life. You gotta get yourself a nice little job at a corner store, serving candy to the kids after school, selling a little drugs on the side... something safe. How long you been on the streets?

ROBBIE   Not counting down-time?

DOUG   Counting everything ... time in the yard, time on the street ... everything.

ROBBIE   Let me see ... thirty, no, thirty-six years, I guess.

DOUG   Jeezus, Robbie. Thirty-six years of putting yourself on the line and nothing to show for it. What a loser.

ROBBIE   Now wait a minute,...

DOUG   Nothing. No house. No woman. No vacations to Florida. Not even a decent car. What a loser.

ROBBIE	(*hesitant*) Now, Dougie, with all respect, I've had not a bad life. Sure I got busted a couple of times too much, but there have been some good times there too.
DOUG	What good times? You wouldn't know a good time if it whacked you in the head. Something I feel like doing again.
ROBBIE	(*desperate to prove himself*) Sure, there were some good times. Lots of them. Why, your mother and me... (*stops himself dead*)
DOUG	What? What did you say, you little sh..../ (*grabs him by the collar*)
ROBBIE	(*overlapping*) nothing./ Dougie, nothing. Just a slip of the tongue.
DOUG	I heard you say 'your mother and me'. Is that not what you said? Isn't it? (*throwing ROBBIE back against in his chair*)
ROBBIE	(*resigned*) Yeah ... yeah.
DOUG	(*standing over him*) That's what you said! That's what you said?
ROBBIE	Yeah, yeah, that's what I said. I said your mother and me. You see, I was goin' tell you sooner or later.
DOUG	Make it sooner.
ROBBIE	Take it easy, Doug. Sit down. I guess I got some explaining to do. I owe you. You see, Irene, your mother, wasn't ... wasn't with a guy in the army who got shot in the leg and died overseas. She was married to me ... who got shot in the leg ... doing time.
DOUG	Oh, jeez ... I'm goin' puke. I don't want to hear the rest of this...

ROBBIE   I promised her I'd take care of you before she
                    died. But, you see, she died before I got out.
                    I figured you were better off with a hero for
                    a dad, than me, so I let the story stick.
                    There was nothin' in it for me, except... (*voice
                    trails off*) And, besides you wouldn't have
                    believed me anyway. You hardly knew me
                    then.

                    I thought maybe we could be pals, a team,
                    score big just once. Live our lives out having
                    great times. We never scored the big one,
                    Doug, but we have had some times. We've
                    done lots of stuff together, more than most
                    dads and their kids.

DOUG   Oh, give it a break. Yeah, like B and E.
                    Dealin'. The odd bank job. Not exactly 'take
                    me out to the ball game.'

ROBBIE   Don't be like that ... son. I woulda gone to a
                    ball game with you, if you'd wanted.

DOUG   (*anger returns*) Don't call me that. Don't call
                    me 'son'. I never wanted you for a dad. I
                    never asked for a loser like you...

                              *DOUG explodes out of his chair and crosses
                              upstage to the door, then he stops to take one
                              look back at his father. ROBBIE doesn't notice
                              — his head is in his hands. As DOUG exits,
                              a siren sounds, far away.*

                                        * * *

Scene 14

from "Dreaming and Duelling"

by *John Lazarus and Joa Lazarus*

1 female / 1 male

PURPLE FACE

    Everyone has at least one part of their appearance that they don't like all that much. In this scene, Louise is a very pretty girl, but has a large, purple birthmark on her face.

    Playing a character with a handicap has given many professional actors memorable performances and earned them awards. Whether it's a limp, like Dustin Hoffman in "Midnight Cowboy", or mental slowness, like Tom Hanks in "Forrest Gump", disabilities require extreme concentration and focus on the part of the actor. Would Louise, consciously or sub-consciously, try to hide her birthmark with her hand? Or sit facing away from the person to whom she was talking? Or, has she learned to live with it and expects others to as well?

    There is also a moment in this scene where a tear would not be out of place. There's no need to squeeze onions before performance to gush Niagara; good actors know that an expression, held a moment, and/or a breaking of the voice and a pause, are all an audience needs to get the right idea. Try it.

    This is the first of two scenes from John Lazarus and Joa Lazarus' marvelous play, "Dreaming and Duelling". If you like its style, check out the other scene in the fourth section when Eric and his friend Joel try a little sword-fighting.

PURPLE FACE

> ERIC is in love with LOUISE, who is very pretty but has a port-wine stain on her face. A boy named Skelly insulted Louise about her birthmark, and ERIC's friend Joel, like ERIC an avid fencer, used the insult as an excuse to start a sword fight with Skelly, which got him expelled from Fencing class. The setting is the school lunchroom.
>
> ERIC and LOUISE are sitting at a table. ERIC has his lunch in front of him and LOUISE is carrying a couple of books. She has come to talk with him.

ERIC   So then Joel's winning, eh? I mean he was really wiping the guy out, it was amazing. I've never seen Skelly lose at anything before.

LOUISE   How exciting.

ERIC   Well, it — well, anyway, then Skelly throws down his épée and says he gives up, and so then Joel goes *really* crazy. And then he tried to hit him with it, and—

LOUISE   What? Wait a minute. Joel tries to hit Skelly *after* he drops his sword?

ERIC   Yeah.

LOUISE   Across the face.

ERIC   Yeah. But anyway, Thorpe stopped him, and that was that.

LOUISE   How did it start?

ERIC: There was this — argument.

LOUISE: About me.

ERIC: Well. Skelly said some more stuff, eh?

LOUISE: I see. So then Joel comes to the rescue? That figures.

ERIC: It happened really fast. I tried to stop it.

LOUISE: Did you, Eric? Did you really?

ERIC: Yeah!

LOUISE: Thorpe managed to stop it.

ERIC: Thorpe is Thorpe. (*brief pause*) Well. Maybe I coulda done better. Maybe I coulda really stepped in there.

LOUISE: Maybe.

ERIC: But I didn't know how serious it was gonna get. I didn't know it would end up with Joel getting kicked out and everything.

LOUISE: Joel getting kicked out! That's what I mean! That's all you think of. What about me, Eric?

ERIC: I thought of you.

LOUISE: Did you think of me turning into the laughing stock of the school? All over again? How long do you think it's gonna take, Eric? Before the word spreads they were fighting over Purple Face? Word's already out. It's gonna be just like it was when I first got here. That's really funny, you know: when I first got here, you and Joel were practically the only people who didn't make a big deal about my skin. And now they're finally getting used to me around here, finally

	treating me like a human being, and look who starts a whole new fuss! That's all they need! Everybody'll be talking about me, they'll start in with the *jokes* — (*brief pause, possibly tears*) Did you think about that? Did you think about what it'll do to me?
ERIC	(*feebly*) I tried to stop them.
LOUISE	I gotta tell you. I'm scared you're gonna get like Joel.
ERIC	How's that?
LOUISE	Insane.
ERIC	Oh, come on, Louise!
LOUISE	Eric, you got to stay away from him for a while. Just avoid him for a while.
ERIC	Avoid Joel.
LOUISE	You hear your tone of voice? It's like I said to do something horrible. Listen, it would be good for you. It might even be good for him.
ERIC	Louise, he's my best friend. He gives me the only real fun in my life. My only fun these days is fencing an' horsing around with Goldner.
LOUISE	Well, that sounds pretty weird right there.
ERIC	Okay, you give me some fun in my life and maybe I'll stay away from Joel.
LOUISE	Go to hell.
ERIC	I'm sorry, I was just kidding.
LOUISE	I don't trade myself
ERIC	I know, I was kidding!

LOUISE	Yeah, right, you were kidding. Exactly. You were kidding just like he does. You learned this garbage from him.
ERIC	I am not like Joel. You're just making something up! Look, did I get in the fight? Did I try and cut up Skelly? Did I get kicked out of Fencing?
LOUISE	No.
ERIC	So I'm a little bit more together than he is, okay?
LOUISE	Okay. I mean, I know that. But I'm just afraid of — (*hesitating*)
ERIC	(*gently*) Yeah, what? You're afraid of...?
LOUISE	I am afraid of losing you as a friend. You are just about my only real — male friend. Every other boy is either — I don't know — they want sex — or they see my skin is weird, so they think I'm all weird... This is embarrassing. (*beat*) I don't want to ask you to choose between me and Joel. But I'm afraid of losing you. And I'm not gonna keep you by having sex with you. And — if you're gonna stay friends with Joel, I don't know what to do.
ERIC	I'm not gonna just dump him. You expect me to just dump him? You think that would be fair?
LOUISE	No. I know.
ERIC	I mean he's got feelings too, you know. He just lost his only fun in life. He isn't just some vicious maniac or something, you know, the guy is hurting.
LOUISE	I know. I know.

* * *

Scene 15

from "Skin"

by Dennis Foon

1 female / 1 male

PHIROZA AND TODD

 Congratulations ! You've picked a winner. This scene is a charmer.

 Phiroza is originally from India, but she has lied - well, sort of, stretched historical truth about her heritage to Todd, a guy she likes, by telling him that her family comes from 'Persia'. She thinks that the truth may change Todd's feelings for her. She has experienced some prejudice at school. But, she's dead wrong about Todd.

 This scene makes audiences laugh if the actor playing Phiroza shows right from her opening **direct address** that she is very nervous (sweaty hands, short breaths), and if the actor playing Todd shows that he may not be as much in the dark as Phiroza thinks. In fact, if Todd lets the audience (but not Phiroza) in on *his* secret early on, then we have a great case of **dramatic irony** - when the audience knows *more* than one of the actors in the scene. **Dramatic irony** has caused more laughter in theatres over the years than any banana peel.

Phiroza and Todd

PHIROZA So Todd kept thinking I was from Persia. But I was really sick of the lie. I had to be so careful about everything I said to him. I wanted him to meet my family — but what if he started asking my dad questions about life in Persia? I decided to tell him the truth — but it wasn't going to be easy.

TODD Hey, Phiroza, where'd you put my Springsteen tape?

PHIROZA hands him a card.

Thanks. What's this? A birth certificate? It's yours. Place of birth Bombay, India. ... I thought you were from Persia.

PHIROZA That's right, we're from Persia.

TODD Then why does it say India?

PHIROZA Because I grew up in India.

TODD It says you were born in India.

PHIROZA I lived in India 'til I was four.

TODD And then you went back to Persia to be born?

PHIROZA No, then I went to Canada.

TODD I thought you said you were from Persia.

PHIROZA I am.

TODD So did you get born twice, once in Persia and once in India?

PHIROZA No.

TODD	Let me see if I've got it. You were born in India, then you came to Canada but you're from Persia.
PHIROZA	You've got it.
TODD	I do? Ever been to Persia?
PHIROZA	Personally?
TODD	Yes, personally.
PHIROZA	I was one of the Parsi people who came from Persia to India.
TODD	When?
PHIROZA	When?
TODD	Yeah, when.
PHIROZA	Oh, about ... *eight (mumbles)* years ago.
TODD	Eight years ago?
PHIROZA	Not exactly.
TODD	Eight how many years ago.
PHIROZA	Hundred.
TODD	Eight hundred years ago? You went from Persia eight hundred years ago and came to India and were born and came to Canada when you were four?
PHIROZA	Because I was born again, like reincarnation.
TODD	I think you're the first older woman I ever went out with.
PHIROZA	I'm the same age as you.

TODD	Right. I see. You were born in this life, so this is the life that counts, right?
PHIROZA	Right.
TODD	So in this life, you were born in India, right?
PHIROZA	... right.
TODD	And in this life, you're Canadian, right?
PHIROZA	Right.
TODD	Right. So that makes you...
PHIROZA	Indo-Canadian.
TODD	Right.
PHIROZA	Right ... sorry for putting you on for so long. I should have told you sooner but the longer I waited, the harder it got to tell you, and I didn't know what to say ... sorry. *(slight pause)* Do you want to break up?
TODD	Nah.
PHIROZA	For sure?
TODD	Yeah ... cause I have a confession to make too.
PHIROZA	You do?
TODD	Yeah.
PHIROZA	What is it?
TODD	Well ... you know I told you I was in Grade Twelve, supposed to graduate this year-
PHIROZA	What grade are you in!
TODD	I was afraid to tell you—

PHIROZA	What grade!
TODD	... Three.
PHIROZA	What? How old are you?
TODD	Seven. You wanna break up?
PHIROZA	Get out of here!
TODD	I am, I'm seven years old. These are new teeth, see?
PHIROZA	You nut!
TODD	You wanna break up?
PHIROZA	No, I like younger men.
TODD	Oh, whew!
PHIROZA	You like older women?
TODD	Oh yeah.
PHIROZA	Whew! *(to audience)* Hey, that wasn't so bad. I could have told him the first day we met. I guess I knew from the start how he felt about me. I just wasn't sure how I felt about myself.

***

Scene 16

from "Carrying the Calf"

by Shirley Barrie

2 females

INDIE

This is the first of two scenes by the prolific Toronto playwright, Shirley Barrie. The other scene, also for two female actors, is in the fourth section ("I Am Marguerite") and is written in a very different style. INDIE is an excerpt from a full-length play for four females (unfortunately, a rare event in theatre) called "Carrying The Calf" which uses the choreography of the *kata* to unify the play. A *kata* is practiced throughout the scene, so find someone who has taken even a single Karate class and ask them to teach you a basic *kata*.

Indira has dragged her West Indian friend, Sharon, 17, along to a karate class because she has been experiencing some violence from 'goons' at school and thinks, at this point, that learning karate is the answer. Self-confident Sharon has picked up karate very fast and advises Indie on moves in the gym, and in her life.

Doing something **physical** (in this case, a *kata*), while **speaking** about something completely different, is a balancing act essential to the skillful actor. This scene provides an excellent opportunity to add this ability to your burgeoning bag of tricks.

"Carrying The Calf" won Shirley Barrie a prestigious Dora Mavor Moore Award in 1992 to add to her many play credits and awards. In addition to playwrighting, she has founded three theatre companies.

INDIE

                    INDIRA enters, obviously upset. She puts down her school bag. The skirt and blouse she's just changed out of are stuffed any old way in the top. She begins to practice the kata with aggression, but she can't get it right and keeps breaking off in frustration. SHARON enters and watches INDIRA.

SHARON   No, Indie. Look. (*demonstrating that she can do it well*)

INDIRA   I did that.

SHARON   And forward.

INDIRA   Oh.

SHARON   And then ... (*finishing*) Do it again. (*as INDIRA starts, she begins to warm up*) I saw your Dad today.

INDIRA   Where?

SHARON   In the store, stupid. Where d'you think? My Mum made me go down for some vacuum cleaner bags ... right before video hits. Usually your old man doesn't say more'n two words to me. But today, when I'm trying to get back for the number two song, he starts giving me the third degree.

                    INDIRA stops the kata.

SHARON   Wants to know how we're getting on with the big project.

INDIRA   He suspects something. I'm dead. What'd you say?

SHARON	What could I say? I couldn't even remember what you said we were supposed to be doing!
INDIRA	"The benefits of physical exercise on the learning process."
SHARON	Oh.
INDIRA	What'd you tell him, Shar...
SHARON	Nothing too...specific. It was a lot of hard work. You know. Stuff like that. Don't worry. I think he bought it.
INDIRA	(*relieved*) You do that real well.
SHARON	What?
INDIRA	Talking a lot to cover up the fact you don't know nothing.
SHARON	(*going after INDIRA half-playfully kicking*) Very funny, Miss-Know-It-All, Do-Nothing.
INDIRA	I was just teasing.
SHARON	I waited for you for two buses after school. Where were you? (*no reply*) Indie?
INDIRA	I was ... in the washroom.
SHARON	(*pause*) Jakey Barnes.
INDIRA	Why is he picking on me?
SHARON	Don't be so dumb, Indie. You're smart, and you wouldn't go out with him and you're brown. You should just tell him to screw off.
INDIRA	I can't, Sharon. Every time I see him I get so scared.
SHARON	All these weeks you been dragging me out here .... haven't you learned anything?

INDIRA Yeah. But...

SHARON Did you think if you came out to this class for a couple of months, all your problems would just — go away. Poof!

INDIRA I guess I wish they would. Yeah.

SHARON Daydreams! Bullies are real, Indie.

INDIRA I know that.

SHARON You're gonna have to tell somebody.

INDIRA No! Look — I told you already, Shar, it'd get back to my Dad. I know it would. And he'd take me right out of school. He'd send me back to India.

SHARON Come on.

INDIRA He's already talking about it.

SHARON Why?

INDIRA Because (*mimicking her father*) "there are no moral standards in this country." There's no sex or drugs in India.

SHARON Yeah?

INDIRA That's what he thinks. I've lived here since I was five years old, Sharon. This is where I want to be.

SHARON Well he can't make you go.

INDIRA Oh no? And even if he didn't he wouldn't let me stay at school. I'd be working in the store. I've got to sort it out on my own.

SHARON So what'd you tell him about the rip in your jacket the other day.

INDIRA	I said I caught it on my locker.
SHARON	Yeah, well just remember, I won't be around to get you out of trouble next year.
INDIRA	You got the job!
SHARON	No.
INDIRA	Maybe you will end up back at school.
SHARON	I'm not that desperate. But my parents're getting really mean. If I'm not at school they're gonna make me pay a fortune in rent.
INDIRA	So why don't you stay in school.
SHARON	Thank you, Firoza.
INDIRA	This doesn't have anything to do with her. For four years all you've talked about is going to college and being a fashion designer. And now it's like you're giving it all up 'cause some stupid counsellor gets up your nose.
SHARON	Just bug off, alright. (*pause*) God, I'm glad this stupid course is nearly finished.
INDIRA	I thought you were enjoying it.
SHARON	Huh!
INDIRA	You're the best one of all of us.
SHARON	Yeah. I know. But it makes me feel funny.
INDIRA	What d'you mean?
SHARON	I don't know. Just funny. I don't like it.
INDIRA	You mean Calvin doesn't like it. (*as SHARON looks at her*) Are you gonna wait while I change tonight?

SHARON   You were taking too long.

INDIRA   Firoza was loaning me the calendar for her university. And I wasn't that long!

SHARON   Calvin was getting restless. You know what he's like. It's weird, eh? All this time we've been going out he was always busy on Tuesdays. All of a sudden he's free — every damn Tuesday he's waiting for me, and I'm all hot and smelling like the school changing room. Chuh! (*looking in her bag*) I knew it! I forgot my deodorant. Have you got any, Indie?

INDIRA   I'm not meeting anybody after, am I? Anyways I use the smell to keep people away when I have to walk home on my own.

                INDIRA goes after SHARON, arm up. They play out a smell/repel routine.

                I scare off attackers.

SHARON   Nooo. Help! It's an offensive weapon.

INDIRA   But legal. Ha, ha. (*surprising SHARON with a hold and flip*)

SHARON   (*leaping up on the attack and then softening*) That was pretty good, Indie. (*laughing together*) You'll do.

INDIRA   No I won't....

SHARON   Indira!

INDIRA   I'm not scared of you. I just can't imagine getting close enough to somebody I'm scared of to do that.

SHARON   Hey — those goons at school weren't six feet away when your jacket got "caught on your locker", were they?

INDIRA	No. But...
FIROZA	(*entering*) Hi, girls.
SHARON & INDIRA	Hi.
FIROZA	How's things?
INDIRA	Great!

SHARON looks at INDIRA, sucks her teeth and turns away.

***

Scene 17

"Derailed"

by Emil Sher

2 males

      Derailed, from the play of same name, written by Emil Sher and created by Catherine Hayos and Rena Polley, is a fairly short scene relative to the others in this section, but the characters of Victor, the conductor, and in particular, George, the businessman, must be played with a great deal of energy to make the scene work.

      Emil Sher describes Derailed as **'a stylized comedy noir'** - that means that real people such as businessmen and train conductors have been **exaggerated to the point of comedy** and where they're behaviour shows the world to be a dismal, disintegrating (hence 'black') place.

      Now, how does one show this as an actor? Well, try to be bigger than real life - strut, bellow and scare - if you are George- and if you are playing Victor, try to be clever, doubting and witty - something your average train conductor wouldn't have time for.

      Derailed is set in the corridor of a train, but don't let that fact restrict your movement. Victor should be occupied with storing luggage, checking his timetable, etc. before George's entrance and during the scene. It's Victor's job to **create 'the where'** - show the audience where the scene is set by touching and using objects typically found in that location. Besides, George has his ball to play with.

      If you like this style, try next the scene from George F. Walker's classic **comedy noir**, "Zastrozzi", and prepare to meet "the master criminal of all Europe." It's in the third section and also requires two males.

Derailed

>*This is a stylized comedy noir that involves a train ride, an unscrupulous advertising executive, his wife, his mistress and the conductor who oversees their quirky, bittersweet journey. Set in the confines of a train compartment, the stage set is completely constructed of luggage, weathered trunks and suitcases which delineate the different compartments and occasionally conceal a character. As this odd quartet embark on their voyage, it becomes painfully apparent that their lifelong quest for physical comfort has only resulted in masking their emotional emptiness.*
>
>*Time is the late 1950s. Place is a moving train. Characters are GEORGE, a businessman, and VICTOR, a train conductor.*
>
>*GEORGE meets VICTOR in the corridor.*

GEORGE   Tell me something, Victor. What games did you play as a kid?

VICTOR   I was never a kid.

GEORGE   You were born a conductor?

VICTOR   I had to grow up quickly.

GEORGE   You must have played some games.

VICTOR   Some.

GEORGE   Games with balls?

>*Bounces a ball to VICTOR.*

VICTOR   Sometimes.

GEORGE   How much would you pay for a ball if you were a kid?

VICTOR   I'm not a kid.

Bounces ball back to GEORGE.

GEORGE   More than nickel?

VICTOR   Depends on the ball.

GEORGE   Depends on the kid. Kids have changed, Victor.

VICTOR   Kids are kids.

GEORGE   Times have changed. There's money out there, Victor. Kids with money.

Throws ball to VICTOR.

VICTOR   Kids don't make money.

Throws ball back to GEORGE.

GEORGE   Kids make choices. They want or they don't want. I can make them want. You like kids?

VICTOR   Some.

GEORGE   I love kids. Kids are going to make me rich. Know what success feels like? Here, feel this. *(Placing ball in VICTOR's hand)* Squeeze it. That's the feel of success.

VICTOR   It's a ball.

GEORGE   It's a campaign. It's a billboard. It's a television commercial. I'll package this ball so that every kid in the country wants one for his very own. What do you think of that?

VICTOR   It's still a ball.

GEORGE   It's not a ball! Look, it has a "B" on it.

VICTOR   "B" for ball.

GEORGE   That's right. Simple, isn't it?

VICTOR   Very.

GEORGE   Imagine every kid on the block has a ball with a "B" on it except you. How would that make you feel? I don't give people what they want. I give them what they think they want.

VICTOR   And you think they want a ball with a "B" on it.

GEORGE   Like everyone else, they want to belong. That's what we're selling. The opportunity to belong. *(beat)* Buy a ball and belong.

VICTOR   Catchy slogan.

GEORGE   Just made it up. Know what *slogan* means?

VICTOR   Money.

GEORGE   A war cry. *(bounces ball on VICTOR's chest)* A battle for your mind. There are a million choices out there. How're you going to choose? You can't. I point the way to the needs you never knew you really needed.

VICTOR   If I never knew I needed them, how can they be needs?

GEORGE   We know what we're doing, Victor, and we do it well. So well we're giving money away, for God's sake. To a children's hospital. We're saving children's lives. When was the last time you saved a child's life?

VICTOR   Hasn't happened yet.

GEORGE   I love kids.

                GEORGE throws ball in air. VICTOR catches it.

                        ***

Scene 18

from "Departures and Arrivals"

by Carol Shields

2 characters

ALPHA AND BETA

    After publication of Carol Shields' two blockbuster novels, *The Stone Diaries* (1993), which won the Governor General's Literary Award and the 1995 Pulitzer Prize for Fiction, and her recent novel, *Larry's Party* (1997), also acclaimed around the world, people may have forgotten that she also is an accomplished writer of plays, such as "Departures and Arrivals" (1990), represented here by the hilarious short scene with Alpha and Beta.

    The entire play is set in an airport; this particular scene occurs in front of the luggage chute when Alpha and Beta, "dressed identically and looking androgynous," both reach for two identical bags circling the carousel. And I dare you to read the rest, right now, without laughing out loud.

    This scene is the ultimate example of *implying* meaning without actually *saying* it. Does Carol Shields ever mention the word "sex" in the dialogue? Yet, it is *between the lines* all the way through. Actors call the meaning between (or beneath) the lines **sub-text**, and learning to use **sub-text** is a good actor's bread and butter. It starts with the right **tone**, the right **emphasis**, and the right **pace**, and you can get the audience to think of anything you want!

Alpha and Beta

>*ALPHA and BETA, dressed identically and looking androgynous, start to reach for the bags, then pull back, exchange looks, and then let the cases go around again. They repeat this two or three times, each finally taking one.*

ALPHA   Coincidence.

BETA   Yes. It is.

ALPHA   I've never seen ... one ... like mine before.

BETA   I haven't either. I thought mine was ... the only one ... the only one there was.

ALPHA   That's what I thought too.

BETA   It's not that I haven't looked. I mean ... I really have ... looked ... but I've never seen—

ALPHA   To tell you the truth, I'd given up looking.

BETA   So had I. I was resigned.

ALPHA   Goodness!

BETA   What is it?

ALPHA   How can we be sure ... well, that this is yours and ... this is mine?

BETA   We could always—

ALPHA   Always what?

BETA   Well, I was going to suggest ... I don't want to intrude on ... to be overly personal, but I was going to suggest—

Section Two / 96

ALPHA — Please go ahead. Don't be shy.

BETA — Well, I was going to suggest that ... we ... open them.

ALPHA — Oh, I never open mine. Never.

BETA — I don't either. At least I never have before.

ALPHA — I don't think I could. I'm awfully sorry.

BETA — Have you had yours ... for a long time?

ALPHA — Well, come to think of it, it has been a long time. In fact—

BETA — I've always had mine.

ALPHA — You get so you're attached. *(laughing)* It's not easy ... I mean it's hard to think of not having one.

BETA — I know just what you mean.

ALPHA — I don't even like ... to let anyone else ... touch mine.

BETA — That's how I feel. But the truth is, well—

ALPHA — Well?

BETA — The truth is ... no one's ever touched mine.

ALPHA — Oh. In my case—

BETA — Yes, go on. You can tell me.

ALPHA — Well, the fact is, no one ... no one's ever *wanted* to touch mine.

BETA — No one?

ALPHA — No one.

BETA	Maybe—
ALPHA	Yes?
BETA	Maybe you'd let me ... touch it.
ALPHA	Oh, I don't know.
BETA	Just a little, you know, just a little pat.
ALPHA	Well, I don't suppose ... why not?
BETA	(*touching case*) There.
ALPHA	Oh.
BETA	That wasn't so bad, was it?
ALPHA	No. Not at all. I ... liked it. I enjoyed it.
BETA	That's good.
ALPHA	Would you like me to ... give yours ... just a little pat?
BETA	Do you think you could?
ALPHA	(*touching case*) There. And there.
BETA	Thank you. Very much.
ALPHA	You're welcome.
BETA	I've got an idea.
ALPHA	What?
BETA	No, never mind. Forget what I said.
ALPHA	Please.
BETA	Well, I just thought ... now if you don't like this idea, all you have to do is—

ALPHA	I'll like it. I promise.
BETA	Well, what if I gave you mine ... and you gave me ... yours?
ALPHA	I... I—
BETA	I hope you don't think—
ALPHA	What I was going to say is ... I think that would be wonderful.
BETA	Really?
ALPHA	Really.
BETA	Well, here you are.
ALPHA	And here you are.
BETA	Thank you.
ALPHA	Thank *you*.
BETA	Are you going this way?
ALPHA	Yes, as a matter of fact—
BETA	(*offering an arm*) Well, why don't we—
ALPHA	We might as well.

They exit.

* * *

Scene 19

from "1837 - The Farmer's Revolt"

by Rick Salutin with Paul Thompson

1 female / 1 male

THE PROPOSAL

    Collective Theatre, when actors and director work together to research, improvise and perform an original play, has been called a distinctly Canadian form of drama.

    The following scene is taken from one of the most popular collective creations, called "1837 - The Farmers' Revolt", by one of our most famous collective companies, Toronto's Theatre Passe Muraille. For an all-too-brief time in the 1970's, it brought together the talents of Paul Thompson as director and Rick Salutin as playwright.

    This scene is in an attempt to tell the story of the Mackenzie Rebellion in Upper Canada more than 150 years ago. You may not have been in Upper Canada in 1837 and you may not be a poor, immigrant farmer, but you have been in a social situation where you felt, as Mary and Edward do, "horribly awkward." Before you begin, describe this situation to your partner.

    As you read the scene, pay close attention to the stage directions — writing a scene after creating it makes the **pauses** between the lines very important in achieving the real feeling of the original **improv**.

The Proposal

                EDWARD PETERS, a farmer, is stage left, waiting for someone to arrive. Enter MARY MACDONALD, stage right. She is expecting to be met. She does not notice him. He approaches nervously.

EDWARD   Excuse me, are you Miss Mary MacDonald?

MARY   I am. (*she sounds very Scottish*)

EDWARD   Oh. I'm Edward Peters.

                They are both horribly awkward.

MARY   I'm very pleased to make your acquaintance Mr. Peters.

EDWARD   I'm very pleased to meet you. (a *painful silence*) You must be tired after such a long trip.

MARY   Yes, I am — a bit.

EDWARD   They have benches here for people if you'd care to ... um...

MARY   Oh, thank you.

                They cross and sit down.

EDWARD   (*plunging*) I wrote you a letter, Miss MacDonald. I don't know if you received it, proposing a date for the ... um ... for our wedding.

MARY   (*nearly choking with nervousness*) Yes. I got it.

EDWARD   Ah. Well. Would two weeks be satisfactory then?

MARY	Yes. That would be just fine. I wouldn't want to put you to any trouble.
EDWARD	No. It's no trouble.
	They sit in awful silence. He leans over and away from her to spit,. He notices her watching him and swallows it instead.
MARY	Oh feel free.
EDWARD	Ah, no. I didn't really feel like it.
MARY	It's quite hot, is it not?
EDWARD	Yes. It's usually quite hot here in August. It's going to get *a* lot colder though.
MARY	What kind of farm do you have Mr. Peters?
EDWARD	It's *a good* farm. I raise wheat, built most of a barn, got a good frame house. I think you'll be very comfortable there. Nice furniture. Rough, but it's usable. I built it myself. I'm good with my hands.
MARY	*(trying hopelessly to relax him and herself)* Yes...
EDWARD	And I don't drink.
MARY	*(not really happy about it)* Oh.
EDWARD	I bought a cow.
MARY	You did—
EDWARD	Yes, I thought you'd be used to fresh milk so I went and bought a cow.
MARY	*(pleased)* And what's her name?
EDWARD	*(embarrassed again)* Cow.

MARY	Cow?
EDWARD	Well when you only have one, you just ... call *it* ... cow ....
MARY	*(feeling their failure to communicae)* Oh...
EDWARD	But you could go ahead and give her a nice name.
MARY	I could?
EDWARD	Sure. You'll be milking her and looking after her. You could go ahead and name her.
MARY	Thank you.
EDWARD	You're welcome.

With great relief he spots someone coming.

That's George. See that big fellow on the wagon there? That's my brother, George. He's come down to take us back to the farm.

MARY	Now?
EDWARD	Yes.

They start across the stage. MARY is in front of EDWARD. MARY stumbles and almost falls. EDWARD catches her by the arm. it is the first time they've touched. They smile.

EDWARD	You've got to watch where you're walking, Mary. There's ruts.
MARY	Yes.

They go off together.

* * *

Scene 20

from "Secrets"

by John Lazarus

2 females

TOTAL COMMITMENT

  Asides are just an older, shorter version of the stage technique of **direct address**. In this scene, another from John Lazarus' excellent play called "Secrets", Susan and Binnie, frequently use the **aside** to tell the audience what they are 'really thinking' as they talk about Binnie's wild boyfriend, Rocky.

  Restoration actors of the 1700's, who invented the technique of **asides**, used to walk **downstage** while the scene froze behind them and whisper the line at the audience. You don't have to be so stylized. Just don't have your partner **react** at all to your aside, and make it the only time you look directly at your audience. Also, the actor who is *not* giving the aside can use this time to show how she is really feeling, just as you would in a situation like this one when the person you were talking to was momentarily turned away.

  It is traditional to indicate the beginning of an aside with the stage direction (aside). In "Secrets", the playwright has also added the stage direction (*in*) to indicate when the character rejoins the scene.

Total Commitment

          The setting is the school at lunch hour. SUSAN and BINNIE are best friends. This play uses the old convention of "Asides" to tell us what the characters are thinking and give us extra information.

BINNIE   (*off*) Susan!

SUSAN   Yo, Binnie!

BINNIE   (*enters, carrying two bags, hers and ROCKY's*) Hey, how ya doin'?

SUSAN   Same old same old.

    (*sitting*) Gee, that's funny, me too. (*taking out makeup or hairbrush; offering makeup*) Want some?

SUSAN   No thanks, I'm trying to cut down.

BINNIE   (*grooming*) So I heard you got kicked out of English Lit today.

SUSAN   Yeah, I expressed an opinion.

BINNIE   Oh Susan, gotta stop doin' that. This is school.

SUSAN   I know. Bad habit. (*observes BINNIE'S bags*) Jeez, you're looking like a keener today. Two book bags.

BINNIE   Oh, yeah. This one's Rocky's. He left it at my place last night.

SUSAN	(*aside*) Rocky's Binnie's boy friend. Her mother found out they're making love, and she freaked out. (*in*) Your mother let him in the house?
BINNIE	Well, we kind of sorted that out. I told her we're engaged to be married, an' faithful to each other, an' into safe sex. Finally I said she might as well get used to it, 'cause I'm never gonna be a virgin again.
SUSAN	That's not bad.
BINNIE	Yeah, she cried for a while an' then she calmed down. So he was over last night, and he's coming to pick me up tonight and stuff. You are going to this party at Victor's?
SUSAN	No.
BINNIE	No? Everybody's going. I thought one of the guys invited you.
SUSAN	Three of the guys invited me. All for the same reason. So I said no.
BINNIE	Was one of them Victor?
SUSAN	No. Why? (*aside*) Victor's this slightly weird intellectual kind of guy who doesn't fit in any of the regular groups. A little like me. He's nice — fairly cute in his own way — but everybody's saying he's — (*in*) Haven't you heard this rumour going around about Victor?
BINNIE	You mean this thing that he's supposed to be gay?
SUSAN	Yeah.
BINNIE	Yeah, I heard that. It's not true.
SUSAN	Well, he didn't ask me.

BINNIE   And you don't want to go alone?

SUSAN   When I go alone, they say things behind my back, and they all hit on me and grab me and stuff.

BINNIE   Susan, that is grim.

SUSAN   No, really? (*re ROCKY's bag*) Hey, y'ever wonder what Rocky carries around in there?

BINNIE   Why — textbooks and homework.

BINNIE
& SUSAN   (*together*) Not!

BINNIE   Actually it's prob'ly all car parts an' porno mags.

SUSAN   No doubt.

BINNIE   No, wait, let's be fair, he does have a couple of books. 'Cause Victor's helping him on math.

SUSAN   Come on, Bin. I dare ya.

BINNIE   Forget it! Rocky an' I made a solemn pact. We swore we'd respect each other's privacy.

SUSAN   Oh, really? Oh, really? Like the night we found him outside your window?

BINNIE   That was a joke.

SUSAN   So's this.

BINNIE   He was just doing that to be obnoxious.

SUSAN   So are we.

BINNIE   (*pause*) All right.

SUSAN   All right!

They dig through ROCKY's bag. They take out some small car parts, a couple of textbooks, and a "Penthouse".

BINNIE — What'd I tell you?

SUSAN — You know your man, I'll give you that. Whoa! You still writing him love notes after all these years? (*taking out a sheet of paper with computer-graphics hearts and flowers, and typing*)

BINNIE — No. "Dear Rocky."

SUSAN — "Thank you for an unforgettable evening."

BINNIE — "Let it...

SUSAN — "...be our little secret. Hugs and kisses — and wild animal cries — Your Secret Squeeze." (*silence, aside*) Oh, man...

BINNIE — Well, it's a joke.

SUSAN — Well, of course it is.

BINNIE — Prob'ly from one of the guys in Computer Science. Prob'ly Victor. Doing one of his little pretend jokes. (*aside*) I hope.

SUSAN — Well, sure. Look, everything's spelled right, it *must* be Victor. (*aside*) Maybe.

BINNIE — Well! Better put this back. (*stuffs everything back into bag*)

SUSAN — You gonna ask him about it?

BINNIE — Are you kidding? How can I ask without telling him we were snooping?

SUSAN — (*aside*) Oh, God, she really does suspect something.

BINNIE   And I mean, anyway, there's nothing to ask. It's a joke, that's all. 'Cause everybody knows me and Rocky have total commitment.

SUSAN   Well, right, of course. (*aside*) Except you keep hearing things... (*in*) Listen, I'm late, I gotta go. But, you know, if you want to talk or whatever.

BINNIE   What about? (*beat*) Okay. Thanks. I'll see ya tonight at the party, okay? Are you coming, or what?

SUSAN   I dunno.

BINNIE   Come with me an' Rocky. We'll protect you from the heavy hitters.

SUSAN   Well, we'll see. Take it easy, Bin.

                  SUSAN exits.

BINNIE   (*to audience*) That's what I get for looking for stuff. I find stuff.

* * *

Scene 21

from "Liars"

by Dennis Foon

2 males

JACE

Jace's father has been an alcoholic for years. Jace, too, has some of his father's urge to self-destruct, but is on a recent high, inspired by his attraction to Lenny, an apparently perfect girl in his class. In the full version of "Liars", Jace realizes that Lenny also has to deal with the ever-changing demands of an alcoholic parent.

Obviously, not a comic play. But the realism of this scene — Jace has to humour his father, but finally has taken, or given, enough — is what makes it compelling drama, and a challenge to act.

If you choose the role of the drunken father, remember this is not *comic drunkenness*, but the dramatic kind. The key to playing a drunk is to realize, as Michael Caine has said, that they are *not* trying to act as if they are impaired; rather, a drunken character is desperately trying to *appear* sober, but cannot. Understand this distinction, and practice it, before attempting the scene.

JACE

                    JACE's house. FATHER's theme music is playing, perhaps Charlie Pride's "Kiss an Angel Good Morning".

                    FATHER enters with dummy of himself and singing along with the music. (In the original production the actors used mannequins.) He sits, picks up a small television set, starts fiddling with the back of it.

JACE	Yoo hoo! Anyone home? Hi Dad, how ya doing?
FATHER	What'd you do with the screwdriver?
JACE	Nothing. I didn't see it.
FATHER	I'm fixing the TV set. Get me the screwdriver.
JACE	Did you look in the tool box?
FATHER	Of course I looked in the tool box, you idiot. Where else would I look?
JACE	I don't know.
FATHER	Where's you put it!
JACE	What're you asking me for, I didn't touch it.
FATHER	Get me that screwdriver and my beer, right now.
JACE	All right, all right.

                    JACE comes back with the screwdriver and beer.

FATHER All right, that's my kid- Good work, boy. Two things a guy's gotta have. His beer and his screwdriver. Aren't you gonna have one!

JACE Not right now.

FATHER What's with you Jace, won't have a beer with the old man?

JACE Okay.

FATHER Atta boy. You're a good kid, Jace. You're all right. You found my screwdriver. Where was it?

JACE In the toolbox.

FATHER Right where I said it would be. Didn't I? Didn't I tell you where it was?

JACE It was right where you said it would be ... Dad—

FATHER Yeah, what is it, I'm all ears.

JACE I wanna ask a favour...

FATHER Sure, what is it, son — you name it.

JACE Can I have the car Saturday night?

FATHER The car? You wanna borrow the car? Saturday night?

JACE Yeah.

FATHER No problem. It's all yours. I'm not using it. What's mine is yours, kid.

JACE Thanks.

FATHER You're very welcome. So what are you up to?

JACE Gotta date.

FATHER   Oh yeah? Somebody new?

JACE   Yeah. Her name's Leonore. But I call her Lenny.

FATHER   Hey, I think you like this girl.

JACE   She's all right.

FATHER   Just like your old man, playing it cool — but I bet you got goosebumps lining your stomach.

They both laugh.

JACE   You think she knows I'm nervous?

FATHER   Doesn't matter, she'll like you for who you are.

JACE   I guess so.

FATHER   No sweat.

JACE   All right.

They slap hands. Pause. FATHER takes a long drink of his beer, then crushes the can.

FATHER   Where's my screwdriver?

JACE   You just had it.

FATHER   What are you talking about? Where is it?

JACE   It was right there.

FATHER   Don't give me that crap, where'd you put it?

JACE   Here it is.

FATHER   You're always losing my stuff. That time you took my razor.

JACE   I was five years old.

FATHER	You steal my stuff.
JACE	I didn't know what I was doing.
FATHER	You never know what you're doing. How're you gonna make it in this world if you don't take responsibility!
JACE	I was five.
FATHER	How'm I supposed to shave without my razor? Get your own damn razor!
JACE	I've got my own razor, I don't need yours.
FATHER	You just stay outta my stuff. I don't do enough for you, you take everything? I looked all over the house for that damn razor. I was late for the interview. I didn't get the job. How'm I supposed to get work if everybody's always losing my stuff?
JACE	I didn't do anything.
FATHER	Get outta here. Get out! *(shoves JACE)*
JACE	You stupid drunk.
FATHER	What'd you call me?
JACE	You heard me.
FATHER	Come here and say it to me.

Pause. JACE exits.

Where's my screwdriver!

Music.

***

Scene 22

from "Thin Ice"

by Beverley Cooper & Banuta Rubess

2 females / 2 males

PENTHOUSE MAGAZINE

    The characters in this scene are described in the full version of "Thin Ice" in this way:

TONY	a brash and cocky kid, about 17
DES	shy, but tries to be tough
TRISH	flashy dresser, fascinated with sex, self-assured, 16
JENNIFER	fun, a bit shy, inexperienced, 16

    You can have more fun in your group if the actors who are normally more like Des and Jennifer opt to play Tony and Trish, and visa versa. However the group decides to play it, the scene doesn't work nearly as well without the **hand props**. Get two magazines (not necessarily "Penthouse" — a good actor can make a comic book look like "Penthouse" with the right reactions) the napkin, the milkshake and the chips (use cardboard ones - they smell better after a long rehearsal). And, practice Trish's chip spill **beat** separately, or it will not look good.

    The most interesting part of the scene is the **beat** preceding the chip spill when the two conversations are happening at once. Conversation the audience *doesn't* hear is as important in this scene as the dating dialogue they do hear. It doesn't matter *what* you say (and, after many performances, experienced actors have fun saying almost anything during these times) as long as it *looks* as if the two are getting acquainted. This scene is rewarding, and takes a lot of rehearsal.

PENTHOUSE MAGAZINE

The school cafeteria. DES brings a tray over to the table. TONY enters.

TONY: Ahhh, man, I don't believe it. We had a major Math test today. Then they laid all this class project stuff on us in Geography.

DES: Times are tough.

TONY: So — coming to my party?

DES: Wouldn't miss it for anything. I haven't had a blowout since Ratbag's house was set on fire.

TONY: So ... you going with anybody?

DES: Naw.

TONY: You should ask Trish Davies to come with you.

DES: Trish? Why Trish?

TONY: Why Trish? I can't believe you're asking me. Are you blind, man? Haven't you noticed the way she feels about you? I'm serious, I'm dead serious. You were walking down the hall, and she gave you a look — whoo! You should ask her out.

DES: You think that ... uh...

TONY: Yeah.

DES: I hardly ever talk to her.

TONY: Smell the coffee, man. The girl is after you. You married or what?

DES   Why is this so important to you? What's going on here?

TONY   I want a certain person to come to this party and she needs a little encouragement so don't ask any more questions and just pay attention to Trish, O.K.? You like her, doncha?

DES   So who's the certain person?

TONY   You'll see. She's a 10. O.K., a 9.8 and a half.

DES   I can't wait. (*pause*) So I brought the latest edition of *Omni* magazine. Cough up the goods.

TONY   I've got it right here.

> *TONY looks around surreptitiously, then pulls out a "Penthouse". They put it inside the "Omni" and start looking at it.*

TONY   Just look at those molecules.

DES   Good thing you're a science major.

> *They both laugh. JENNIFER enters with a tray. DES shoves the magazines underneath the table.*

TONY   Hey, Jennifer!

JENNIFER   Hi ... I've got some friends sitting over there...

TONY   No, no, I insist. Take a seat, Florence Nightingale. This woman saved my life.

JENNIFER   (*laughing*) Come on.

DES   What's that?

JENNIFER   Milkshake.

DES   You call that lunch?

JENNIFER   I'm on a diet.

            TRISH enters with fries and hamburger.

TRISH   Oh hi. Oh my God, I know I failed. Mr. Wilson is always giving me the hairy eyeball. He's got it in for me.

DES   Hey Trish. Where did you get that outfit?

TRISH   What — these old things?

            TRISH is wearing tight jeans. She gets up and smoothes them down, essentially showing her bum.

TONY   So, Jennifer, have you ever been on a motorbike?

JENNIFER   Yeah, my sister has one.

TONY   You're kidding.

            They engage in conversation, not audible.

DES   So, Trish ... do you go to parties and stuff?

TRISH   Sure, all the time.

DES   I'm just wondering.

TRISH   Trying to ask me out, Des?

DES   No. Yeah. I don't know.

            They continue to have a conversation which the audience does not hear. DES keeps glancing at TONY.

TONY   (*to JENNIFER*) About the party ... like you don't have to come if you have something better to do. I'm sure there are some really great re-runs on TV or something. I mean everyone else is going to be there. Trish is

	coming. I thought you were a good friend of hers.
JENNIFER	Trish is going?
	They continue sotto voce.
DES	Hey, I'm not talking just any pizza joint, O.K., you come with me, you're talking class.
TRISH	(*á la Mae West*) Sure, stranger, I'll come and dine with you.
	DES and TRISH suddenly burst out laughing, and wink at each other.
TONY	What's going on? You guys using sign language? This a private party?
TRISH	Listen Des, you look like a pretty cool type. Why are you hanging out with this loser.
TONY	Oh, excuuuuuuuuse me!
DES	Can I have a fry?
TRISH	Sure take them all. They're really greasy.
	She passes them and they fall on DES's lap.
TRISH	Oh I'm sorry. I'm so embarrassed.
DES	That's O.K.
TRISH	Listen I'll pay for the dry-cleaning —
	DES throws a fry at her.
DES	It's alright, already.
	TRISH throws a napkin at DES.
TRISH	Here's a napkin.

DES	(*throwing it back*) I don't need it.
	The napkin hits JENNIFER. She threatens DES with her milkshake.
TONY	Kids, kids.
	TRISH goes to pick the napkin up off the floor.
TONY	What're you doin' down there, Trish?
TRISH	Ah gross, look what I found under the table (*producing a "Penthouse"*)
JENNIFER	Ugh. You have to be sicko to like that stuff.
TONY	I guess I should be committed to the asylum.
TRISH	I'd love to see you spread-eagled too. Or tied to the front of the car like that. Look at that one. It looks like torture.
TONY	Call Amnesty International.
DES	Give it to me, this is man stuff.
TRISH	Get back to The Middle Ages.
DES	C'mon there's nothing wrong with this.
TRISH	You're brainwashed.
TONY	(*brainwashed voice*) Give me the magazine, I need the magazine.
JENNIFER	You can have it. (*looking at watch*) Time for biology. We're dissecting a frog.
TONY	Now that's sick.
JENNIFER	I love it. Num num.

* * *

Scene 23

from "Secrets"

by John Lazarus

1 female / 1 male

COOL

This scene uses the **aside** to convey much of the **subtext**, or what the characters are *really* thinking. See the intro to Scene 20, TOTAL COMMITMENT, for more explanation of this technique.

Both Victor and Susan have 'reputations' they would like the world to forget. Victor is less experienced than Susan in dating, and thus appears shy as they try to come to an agreement about Victor's party tonight. Susan, as you will see, is much more self-confident.

You can picture the **asides** as being said when you are 'wearing a different mask' than the one used in the social conversation. The **asides** are your characters' real emotions at the time. See if you can change the **tone** of your voice to give the audience the correct impression that the **aside** is the 'real you' talking.

COOL

> *The setting is the school at lunch hour. VICTOR has a crush on SUSAN. VICTOR has a false reputation for being gay; SUSAN has a false reputation for being promiscuous. The play uses the old convention of "asides" to tell us what the characters are thinking and give us extra information.*
>
> *SUSAN enters. VICTOR intercepts her.*

VICTOR   Hey! Susan! How ya doin'.

SUSAN   Okay.

VICTOR   (*nodding*) Cool.

SUSAN   (*aside*) Oh, please.

VICTOR   (*aside*) Oh, help. (*in*) Uh, were you figuring on coming to my party tonight?

SUSAN   No.

VICTOR   Oh. (*aside*) Well, that broke the ice. Okay, here goes. (*in*) Well, I was wondering if you would like to, uh — Whether you would care to, uh...

SUSAN   (*aside*) I hate this stuff.

VICTOR   How would you feel about attending this little soirée as my personal date? (*aside, wincing*) "Soirée"!

SUSAN   Why?

VICTOR	"Why"? (*aside*) What does she mean, "Why"? (*in*) What do you mean, "Why"? For — you know, for fun. For the pleasure of each other's company. (*aside*) Because I'm madly in love with you. (*in*) Just for the heck of it, how's that?
SUSAN	Good reason.
VICTOR	So? What do you say?
SUSAN	(*aside*) If it's true he's gay, then why is he— Oh, of course. (*in*) First I want you to tell me your real reason.
VICTOR	What? What do you mean? (*aside*) Does everybody know how I feel?
SUSAN	Well — Victor — look, you're inviting me because of this rumour that you're gay, aren't you?
VICTOR	(*aside*) Gets fight to the point, doesn't she? (*in*) No! I'm inviting you because I really— Uh...
SUSAN	You want to kind of make a statement.
VICTOR	Yeah. But also — I mean if I gotta invite some girl, it might as well be you. (*aside*) Well, that swept her off her feet. End of dream. (*in*) Well, thanks for considering it, anyway.
SUSAN	Just a minute. I didn't say no.
VICTOR	You mean you're saying yes?
SUSAN	I'm thinking.
VICTOR	Oh. (*aside*) What's she got to think about? Why doesn't she just laugh in my face, kick me in the testicles and get it over with?

SUSAN (*aside*) See, if I go as his date, they'll all make jokes. But also, they won't be leaning on me all night. And Victor seems pretty safe.

VICTOR (*aside*) Everybody says she jumps into bed with a guy if he buys her a drink. I don't believe that, but— Me, she has to go into heavy meditation before she'll decide to spend an evening standing next to.

SUSAN (*aside*) And wouldn't it be nice to have a date with a guy who isn't grabbing and groping and expecting me to— (*in*) Victor, I'd love to be your date this evening. Thank you for asking me.

VICTOR What? Wow. Great. That's great. I — that's just — that's just great. OK thank you.

SUSAN Okay.

VICTOR No, I mean it, you don't know — Thank you.

SUSAN Victor, we don't have to pretend this date is something it isn't.

VICTOR No. (*aside*) What?

SUSAN I mean, I know it's just to shut them all up.

VICTOR Well, it isn't entirely—

SUSAN I can understand if you've had enough of that stuff. I do think what you've already done was very brave.

VICTOR Thank you! (*aside*) She thinks I'm brave! What the heck is she talking about? (*in*) What was brave?

SUSAN   Well, that letter to the school paper defending that boy in Grade Eleven, you know, the, uh...

VICTOR   The homosexual.

SUSAN   Yeah. Which made it pretty obvious, you know, that, uh...

VICTOR   That I'm ... that I'm...

SUSAN   Well, yeah.

VICTOR   Gay.

SUSAN   Yeah.

VICTOR   I'm not.

SUSAN   You're not?

VICTOR   Absolutely not, Susan. And yes, I'm sure.

SUSAN   Oh! Well. Okay. There you go.

VICTOR   You thought I was?

SUSAN   Well, uh...

VICTOR   Susan, I wrote the letter because I happen to not think it's a crime if somebody's gay. Somebody else. It doesn't mean I'm one!

SUSAN   Oh, well, that's nice.

VICTOR   Listen. There's obviously been a little misunderstanding here. If you want to change your mind—

SUSAN   No! No. I said I'd go out with you tonight, and I will.

VICTOR	(*aside*) Oh, great, she's dating me 'cause she has to. Perfect. (*in*) Well, I appreciate that, Susan. Thank you.
SUSAN	My pleasure.
VICTOR	(*aside*) How do you get back to small talk from here?
SUSAN	(*aside*) This is getting highly strained. I'm outta here. (*in*) Well. See you tonight.
VICTOR	Okay. Great. See you tonight.

She exits. VICTOR remains.

VICTOR	(*to audience*) She's going in my direction. But I can't go with her now, you know, it would seem kind of weird, so I have to wait here for a while so I won't be schlepping down the street a half a block behind her. 'Cause that wouldn't be cool.

***

Section Three — THREE TO GET READY

No doubt by now you've realized that rehearsing a scene is like building a good pizza: **memorizing** the lines creates a solid crust which holds all the other stage goodies, such as **character** (the pepperoni, of course), **stage movement and pace** (the smooth and tasty mozzarella), and the **technical effects** (green pepper and onions?).

But, back to the crust. No one likes a soggy, half-baked bunch of cues, least of all your partner when his/her lines are perfect. The scripts in this section are roughly two pages longer than in SECTION TWO (except for the last three — but these have other challenges) so make sure your crust is firm and solid before adding the toppings..

For two girls, try reading Irene Watts' funny and moving piece, "Solo", without getting choked up - I couldn't. For two guys, the scene to start with is I'VE DONE IT! by John Lazarus. Rocky gives his good bud, Victor, some timely advice on his love life. If you're paired with a member of the opposite gender, then try the roles of Jace (the guy) and Lenny (the girl) in an final scene from John Lazarus' wonderful play, "Liars". It's divided into two parts, TRUTH (Scene 26) is followed by ...OR DARE (Scene 27) so you can play either one, or the whole scene if you really want to impress. (Go for it - all that's left out is the short flashback - Jace with his Dad, Lenny with her Mom - which separates TRUTH from ...OR DARE in the full version of "Liars".) Or, if you simply feel like shooting your partner sometimes, try Ragna Goodwin's winner, BUSTER - it's full of murder and other surprises.

Good at accents? Jolly good, old chap, try a British **dialect** in the scene about how our World War One flying ace, Billy Bishop, got his wings. Or, for something completely different, read the words from New Canadian Kid out loud. Finally, if you liked the evil of **comedy noir** in **Derailed**, try playing "Zastrozzi", in THE MASTER CRIMINAL, by Canada's master of **comedy noir**, George F. Walker.

But remember the best pizza has the best crust. Roll, dress and bake at 400 degrees!

Scene 24

"Solo"

by Irene Watts

2 females

    Irene N. Watts is a West Coast writer and director who has worked in many of Canada's established theatres the Neptune, the Citadel, Green Thumb Theatre and The Stratford Festival. Both her scenes in this book were chosen because of the wonderful way she creates a compelling character and story in a short time, expertly drawing the audience into the drama.

    The audience should know within moments of lights up in this scene that something is really bothering Bridget. Her best friend Melissa's flamboyant **character** offers a necessary balance in this moving scene. But, Melissa is also a good listener, and soon settles down to see what is bothering Bridget.

    It's Bridget's story that is the centre of this scene, so the actor must **'take the focus'** during this beat, and give Bridget's **monologues** the spotlight. Watts has cleverly given Melissa the job of reading the letter, not Bridget, so we can watch her face while her best friend reads with emotion. This is a fine moment for both actors and should be rehearsed on its own.

    Yes, Melissa, you can take the written letter on stage with you and read it rather than memorizing, but that's not the way professional actors do it. They memorize. It gives you more control over the **pace** and **emphasis**; two skills that are more closely associated with the ear of the listener, than the eye of the reader.

Solo

Bridget Farrell. Age 13.

Melissa Jones, her best friend. Age 13.

May 1998. The change room of the school gymnasium. BRIDGET FARRELL is hunched on a bench in the far corner, her flute case beside her. The buzzer has just rung for the last period before lunch. The door opens and MELISSA JONES enters. She puts her violin case down.

MELISSA   Thought as much. Hiding. Didn't you hear the buzzer? Dumb question. Bridget Jane Farrell you're gonna be in big trouble. One more absence without a great reason and you're out.

BRIDGET   Sez who?

MELISSA   Mr. James. I covered for you last practice. We won't get away with it again.

BRIDGET   What makes you think I care about the stupid concert and his stupid trip to Montreal?

MELISSA   Because we both know you're dying to go, because you'd be green if one of the other flautists took your spot. So smarten up.

BRIDGET   So time you stopped sneaking around following me. You've been doing it since kindergarten. Get out before someone comes in.

MELISSA   Fine, if that's how you feel.

BRIDGET   That's exactly how I feel. Now beat it.

MELISSA *(sighs dramatically)* Well I guess I'll be rooming in Montreal with that stuck up Sheryll Northey. I'll have to listen to her rhapsodize over Peter Fisher — Rhapsody in blue — get it? You know how she always wears baby blue.

BRIDGET groans, MELISSA mimics Sheryll.

Don't you just love the way his eyelashes curl? He's *so* divine. *(beat)* "Si beau" she's brushing up for her French for Quebec. I'll be too sick to my stomach to even attend the concert let alone play.

MELISSA takes out her violin and plays a few mournful chords. BRIDGET's shoulders begin to shake and she finally bursts out laughing. MELISSA returns the violin to its case.

That's more like it. Bridget, on my knees I'm pleading with you. We're only a few minutes late, we'll dream up an excuse on the way.

MELISSA pulls BRIDGET to her feet.

BRIDGET   I can't.

MELISSA   You can. Why can't you?

BRIDGET   My mom's pregnant.

MELISSA   Your Mom! But she's old, I mean oops, I mean she can' t can she? Oh my gosh, you know what I'm trying to say.

BRIDGET   Your words are music to my ears. Mel, I'll be almost fourteen when it makes its debut.

MELISSA   You're sure? Maybe you misunderstood? *(the girls look at each other)* I guess not. That's why you're hiding.

BRIDGET	Well, kinda. Not exactly. I'm not jumping up and down for joy but I guess it's okay.
MELISSA	So then why the big deal about missing practice?
BRIDGET	OK I'll tell you.
MELISSA	About time!
BRIDGET	You'd have to be blind and deaf not to notice something weird going on in our house the last couple of weeks.
MELISSA	Like what?
BRIDGET-	I'm trying to tell you. I thought at first my Mom had some deadly disease, or was going through the change of life or something. You've only got to say the word coffee and she's running to the bathroom throwing up. So when my Dad said "Dress up I'm taking you both to dinner" I got very suspicious. We're not talking McDonalds here. No, very fancy — pink tablecloths, fresh flowers, candles. Not the usual territory. I was halfway through dessert, Death by Chocolate with strawberries, when my Dad says, "Budgie, we've got a surprise for you."
MELISSA	Budgie! No one's dared to call you that since grade one.
BRIDGET	It gets worse. My Mom blushes and says "We're having a baby." My spoon clatters on the floor, and I yell "A baby." and everyone looks up, and all these old people smiling, and the waiter, drop-dead gorgeous, says "Congratulations Ma'am." I wanted to die.
MELISSA	Oh my God.

BRIDGET   My Dad said, "Takes your breath away doesn't it, Budgie? We knew how happy you'd be." and they, my Mum and Dad, were holding hands. I was so embarrassed I said an awful thing, "You're too old Mom, or is this one going to be adopted too?" My Mom let go of my Dad's hand, and he put his arm around me and kissed my cheek and said, "No, you're the only one we chose."

I mean why did it all have to be so public, don't they know anything about what I feel?

MELISSA   All parents are weird, no doubt.

BRIDGET   So I ran out, and we drove home, no one said one word. I remembered when I was little I always felt special, kinda proud you know, about being chosen. I always had this picture in my head of a room in the hospital, with rows and rows of little cribs with babies in them, and when they came to me my Dad saying "Wrap her up please, that's the one we'll take home."

BRIDGET blows her nose.

MELISSA   It probably was something like that, I mean they did choose you from thousands of kids. So what happened next?

BRIDGET   Dad put the car away.

MELISSA   You are in serious danger of being hit over the head with a blunt instrument. *(lifting the violin case) Tell* me.

BRIDGET   It gets worse. My Mom puts her head on the kitchen table.

MELISSA   Hope she sat down first.

BRIDGET   Do you want to hear or are you rehearsing for woman comic of the millennium?

MELISSA   Sorry.

BRIDGET   So my Mom's crying and saying "I wanted it to be such a nice surprise, and now it's all gone wrong. I did it all wrong." So I kinda patted her, and said it's a terrific surprise, just a bit of a shock you know Mom, and the restaurant and everything. It'll be great, you're not too old at all and Mel and me will baby-sit.

MELISSA   Thanks a lot. Oh sure, it'll be fun. We'll be able to finance the next bus trip. Is that it? Can we PLEASE go into class or we'll never go any place again.

BRIDGET   Then my Mom gives me this letter, they were going to give it to me at dinner.

    BRIDGET hands MELISSA a blue envelope.

MELISSA   What's it say, they gonna send you back?

BRIDGET   *(seriously)* Not funny. Read.

MELISSA   *(takes out a single sheet of well worn note paper, reads)* "Dear Mr. and Mrs. Farrell,"

    Budge, this is for your Mom and Dad.

BRIDGET   Just read.

MELISSA   "Thanks for the beautiful flowers and the photo. Meredith looks so plump and contented. She gained a lot of weight in six weeks. It was hard to let Merry go. I changed my mind a hundred times before signing the adoption papers. Mike and I broke up, we weren't right for each other, well, not for ever. He's going to university and I'm going back to finish high school, try anyway. Fifteen's too young to take care of a baby. I haven't learnt to take care of myself yet. When Merry's older and can understand, please tell her why I couldn't keep her, tell her it wasn't because I didn't want to. I'll always love her and miss her. I'm grateful to you both because I know you love her too. Sing her a lullaby for me, please.

Good-bye. Thank-you. Mandy."

MELISSA   Do you know how lucky you are?

BRIDGET   I guess so. So do you wanna tell me how I'm gonna get through playing a medley of lullabies without bawling?

MELISSA   Easy. You play it for me at home, and I'll cry and your Mom'll cry and you'll cry, and then we'll have hot chocolate and cookies and it'll all be out of your system and you'll be fine, everybody's going to be fine.

BRIDGET   And Mr. James?

MELISSA   Nothing to it. We'll tell him right now — it's almost the end of the period.

BRIDGET   Tell him what?

MELISSA   The truth idiot. You've had an emotional shock, and you had to work through it privately. You're ready to attend every rehearsal from now on, and would he please overlook your absence. And you know what? It'll work, 'cos its true. Come on, little Budgie.

> BRIDGET'S *mock shout of anger coincides with the buzzer for the end of the period.*

***

Scene 25

from "Secrets"

by John Lazarus

2 males

I'VE DONE IT

This scene has the best opening **beat** of any scene in the book! The actor playing Rocky enters with all the tough-guy character you can muster, and Victor seems to stiffen with fear on hearing Rock's first lines. Now, rehearse the beautiful **comic timing** of the next moment with the long **pause**, the face to face (in profile to the audience, so they can see both) and finally Victor's line. Don't drop **character** until you hear the laughter from the audience, then **transition** smoothly into the relaxed laughter of two friends.

If you haven't performed using **asides** — described in TOTAL COMMITMENT (Scene 20) — read that description first. This is a technique used by John Lazarus throughout "Secrets", from which both these scenes are taken.

Even though both characters are eating lunch, try to find some **movement** in the scene: cross to the garbage can with some wrapping; get a real lunch, and suit it to your character, for another laugh. How would a guy like Rocky *sit* at a lunch table? Not on the seat.

In every good scene, a character learns something new. Victor's new understanding of how others see him is key to our enjoyment of the scene, since this is an experience we've all had. Victor goes through many different emotions on his way to the final line - use **pausing** and **reactions** to *take the audience with you*.

I'VE DONE IT

The setting is the school at lunch hour. VICTOR and ROCKY are incongruous best friends, though it's fun if the audience misunderstands the relationship at the beginning.

This play uses the old convention of "asides" to tell us what the characters are thinking and give us extra information.

VICTOR is sitting eating his lunch. Enter ROCKY behind him, carrying a large chain.

ROCKY   Now let's see. What am I gonna do to Victor today?

VICTOR hears this, sits still.

I think maybe I'll tie one end of this chain 'round his ankles and the other end to my car, and drag him 'round the school a few times. (*coming forward to VICTOR*) So you gonna come quiet, or do I gotta beat the daylights outta ya first?

Pause, face to face.

VICTOR   You never just take me out to dinner any more.

ROCKY tries to keep a straight face, but can't. VICTOR cracks up.

ROCKY   (*shoves him*) Flake off, jerk!

VICTOR   (*shoves back*) Jerk off, flake! (*laughs some more, aside*) I kill myself.

ROCKY	Yeah, yeah, yeah... (*sitting beside VICTOR*) Hey, listen, man, it's one thing to joke around like that when we're hangin' out down the garage. But when you flip your wrists an' stuff at the guys around here, they don't know you're kidding.

VICTOR	Oh, come on!

ROCKY	I'm tellin' you, you keep that stuff goin', it's gonna come back an' get you.

He opens his lunch. They eat.

VICTOR	So where's your books?

ROCKY	What?

VICTOR	We were supposed to work on the math, remember?

ROCKY	Oh, yeah. I left all my stuff at Binnie's last night.

VICTOR	Oh, for Pete's sake. You just missed her. I saw she had your bag, but it didn't register.

ROCKY	Oh, yeah? Where? (*calling*) Binnie!

VICTOR	No, she's gone.

ROCKY	Well, I phoned her this morning an' she said she'd bring it to class.

VICTOR	Hey man, the whole point was to have it *before* class. *Now*. At *lunch* hour. I was gonna save your hide, remember?

ROCKY	Yeah, I know, sorry.

VICTOR	Rocky, I can't help you with this crap if you're not even gonna bring your books. I'm not your mother, okay?

ROCKY	Then stop talkin' like her, okay?
VICTOR	Well, I mean, really.
ROCKY	Do I talk to you like that when I'm givin' you the driving lessons?
VICTOR	No, you scream obscenities at me.
ROCKY	Exactly.

They eat in silence.

(*aside*) Well, the guy's got a right to know. He's gonna find out anyways. (*in*) Look, you gotta knock off jokin' like that, okay? 'Cause ya know what Greg's sayin'?

VICTOR	No, and who cares.
ROCKY	He's tellin' everybody he's wearin' surgical gloves to your party, 'cause he doesn't wanna get AIDS.
VICTOR	What? From who?
ROCKY	From you. Him an' Calvin an' them are goin' around seriously sayin' you're gay. An' people believe 'em.
VICTOR	What? Come on. Nobody believes those guys. Do they? (*no answer*) Really? Are you serious?
ROCKY	It's kind of getting around the school, man.
VICTOR	It is? Why didn't you tell me this?
ROCKY	I am. I been tryin' to.
VICTOR	But — but it's a running gag, it's like somebody doing imitations of, uh...
ROCKY	Not the way they're sayin' it.

VICTOR   Really? This is, like, *widespread*? Girls too?

ROCKY   Girls too.

VICTOR   But it's a joke! Everybody does it! You do those jokes so they'll know you're *not* one! How come when I do it, it means I *am*?

ROCKY   Maybe you're more convincing.

VICTOR   Hey, thanks.

ROCKY   Or maybe 'cause of that letter you wrote to the school paper. About how it's okay to be gay.

VICTOR   That was because of that guy in Grade Eleven who got the spit kicked out of him. All I said was they shouldn't beat him up.

ROCKY   Well, so it means you're big on gay rights.

VICTOR   Yeah, but not for *me*, I'm *straight*! Oh, my God, I bet you're right. How stupid of me, eh? How dare I suggest people should live and let live.

ROCKY   Well, I stood up for ya, man. I told them guys you're my friend and you're one hundred percent hetero.

VICTOR   Really? You said that?

ROCKY   I did. I told 'em you been workin' at the garage, an' that you shoot a good game of golf, you know, all the guy stuff.

VICTOR   Well, thank you, my man. (*ritual handshake*)

ROCKY   Hey. I'll stick by you.

VICTOR   A true friend.

ROCKY	Just 'til they start sayin' I'm one too, an' then I'm outta here.
VICTOR	Oh, great, thanks a lot.
ROCKY	No sweat, man.
VICTOR	Rocky, how am I supposed to fight something like this?
ROCKY	I know. It's rough. But just think how you'd feel if you *were* one. So you couldn't even say you weren't.
VICTOR	If I *were* one, I wouldn't mind them saying so!
ROCKY	You wouldn't? You sure? Like that poor jerk they beat up? How do you think he feels?
VICTOR	Yeah, I guess you're right.
ROCKY	(*aside*) I dunno if I should tell him the other thing. Might just make it worse. Except he oughta know what he's up against here. (*in*) All right, Victor, the other thing those guys are saying is, any guy who hasn't done it by the time he's seventeen must be one.
VICTOR	What? Why does that mean I'm gay?
ROCKY	I know, it's—
VICTOR	I mean, even if I'd never done it, why would that — Who says I haven't done it? I've done it dozens of times!
ROCKY	Well, hey, I know that. (*aside*) Yeah, right. (*in*) Look, Victor, those guys got untreated sewage for brains, everybody knows that.
VICTOR	Why do they think I've never done it?
ROCKY	'Cause nobody knows anybody you've done it *with*.

VICTOR	They were all during summer vacations.
ROCKY	Look, Victor, there's nothing wrong with waiting for the right woman, you know?
VICTOR	I am *not* waiting! I've *done* it! LOTS!
ROCKY	Okay, I'm just sayin'. A guy doesn't have to have sex to be cool—
VICTOR	What is this, Socials Nine?
ROCKY	I'm only sayin', there's lotsa guys around who've never had it, and they're still great guys. You'd be surprised.
VICTOR	Easy for you to say, Leonardo.
ROCKY	Hey. What Binnie and I have is special.
VICTOR	All right. Sorry.
ROCKY	(*aside*) What a liar. He's right. I got no right to preach at him.

ROCKY resumes eating, VICTOR frets.

* * *

Scene 26

from "Liars"

by Dennis Foon

1 female / 1 male

TRUTH

  Ever played Truth or Dare? Well, Jace has a variation on this game and teaches it to his girlfriend, Lenny. Beyond the game, though, is Lenny's deeper truth, one that she's been covering up since she was a kid, just as she has told Jace earlier about Tracy, a 'friend' who has a problem at home. Jace knows what it is because he has a parent who is an alcoholic too, and this fact brings Lenny and Jace together in a real game of truth or dare, begun in this scene and concluded in the scene that follows.

  Both scene 26 and 27 are set in a city park, at night. Some blue **gels** would set this up, with some yellow moonlight at centre - a **warmer gel** than the blue and suited for the romance. If you have the resources to suggest on an **upstage flat** some trees and a lake in the distance - go for it. This would also give Jace a place to momentarily hide from Lenny during the tag game at the start.

  Rehearse the contact scenes until you are both comfortable. Professional actors prepare romantic moments as carefully as they do stage fights, ironically. Each actor must know and be comfortable with every move before you are ready for an audience, so they are the only ones surprised. Since both TRUTH and ...OR DARE are together as Scene Nine in Dennis Foon's "Liars", the climax to the play, why not try to perform them both together? That's worth extra credit in any class!

TRUTH

The lake.

LENNY   Where are we?

JACE   Never been here before?

LENNY   Feels like it's the middle of nowhere.

JACE   It's the middle of the park. Just that it's at night. The night changes things.

LENNY   Yeah.

JACE   What was that! *(sneaks off)*

LENNY   *(looks for him)* What? Jace!

Pause. JACE pokes her. LENNY shrieks.

JACE   Got ya!

LENNY   Don't do that!

JACE   Relax. We're in the city. The worse thing you could meet is a goose with rabies.

LENNY   What's in the knapsack?

JACE   My gear.

LENNY   What gear?

JACE   My personal belongings. The essentials. See?

JACE reaches into the pack and pulls out four black T-shirts, one after the other.

LENNY   ... what are you doing with this stuff?

JACE — I moved out today.

LENNY — You left home? Why?

JACE — My dad and I have philosophical differences. *(shows her the bruise)*

LENNY — Are you okay?

JACE — Oh yeah. I feel no pain.

LENNY — What do you mean?

JACE — I got a little help from my friends.

LENNY — What are you on?

JACE — A little of this, a little of that.

LENNY — Where are you going to stay?

JACE — Here. This is my new place. In fact, you're sitting in the living room.

LENNY — You're really going to live outside?

JACE — The weather's nice. I'll just stash my bag in the brush, nobody'll spot me.

LENNY — What if the weather changes?

JACE — I'll cross that bridge when I come to it. It's no big deal. Your friend Tracy should do the same thing.

LENNY — No, Tracy can still talk to her parents. She's not like you. Anyways, you're crazy.

JACE — No, I'm sane. Staying there is crazy. Sooner or later one of us is gonna get killed.

LENNY — It's that bad.

JACE   I couldn't stand it anymore. He's always out of it. Never there. Killing himself and dragging me down with him. I had to get out of there... Let's play something.

LENNY   What?

JACE   Tag.

LENNY   It's too dark.

JACE   *(tagging her)* You're it!

> He runs away. LENNY pauses, then joins the chase. She tags him.

LENNY   You're it!

JACE   *(chasing and tagging her)* You're it!

> JACE runs away, then hides, thinking he's safe. LENNY sneaks up and pokes him in the ribs.

LENNY   You're it!

> JACE shrieks. They laugh.

JACE   What do you wanna play now?

LENNY   Is this what you do on dates? Play kids' games?

JACE   Yeah, why not? I got it. Truth, Dare, Double Dare. Ever played it?

LENNY   No, what is it?

JACE   *(gleefully)* You never played it?

LENNY   No.

JACE	Okay, we take turns, you pick one. If you pick Truth, you have to answer any question I ask and you have to be honest. If you pick Dare, you have to do whatever I say.
LENNY	I don't think I like this game.
JACE	Don't worry, no weird stuff, okay? If you pick Double Dare it's not as outrageous as Dare, but you have to do it twice. What do you say?
LENNY	I don't know.
JACE	Come on, it won't kill you. You start. Truth, Dare, Double Dare.
LENNY	What?
JACE	Pick one.
LENNY	Pick one?
JACE	Truth, Dare, Double Dare.
LENNY	Double Dare.
JACE	Okay. I double dare you to yell, "I've got runny zits."
LENNY	What!
JACE	As loud as you can. Twice.
LENNY	You're kidding.
JACE	Come on. Do it!
LENNY	I've got runny zits!
JACE	Again. Louder.
LENNY	*(yells)* I've got runny zits!

JACE	Don't tell me your problems. Okay, now it's my turn.
LENNY	Truth, Dare, Double Dare.
JACE	Dare.
LENNY	... I can't think of one.
JACE	Dare me to take off my clothes.
LENNY	No way! Swim across the lake and back.
JACE	I can't.
LENNY	I did it. Now it's your turn.
JACE	But I can't swim. Well, I guess you have to punish me.
LENNY	Punish you?
JACE	The punishment is you have to spank me.
LENNY	What?
JACE	Those are the rules. Don't blame me, I didn't make them up.
LENNY	Then who did?
JACE	Mr. Rogers.
LENNY	I'm not going to spank you.
JACE	Sorry, you have to. The rules.
LENNY	No!

JACE lays across her legs.

JACE	Spank!

LENNY lightly spanks him once. He gets up.

Now it's your turn. Truth, Dare, Double Dare?

LENNY   Dare.

JACE   Swim across the lake.

LENNY   I'm not swimming across the lake.

JACE   Punishment.

LENNY   No!

JACE   Mr. Rogers'll come and chop you up in little pieces!

LENNY   Okay, okay.

She lies across his legs. He lightly spanks her once.

Truth, Dare, Double Dare.

JACE   Truth.

LENNY   Why did your dad hit you?

JACE   He said I could have the car, but he forgot, as always. I got mad, we got into a fight. He hit me... Truth, Dare, Double Dare.

LENNY   Truth.

JACE   Are you Tracy?

LENNY   What?

JACE   Your friend Tracy is really you. True?

Pause.

LENNY   How did you know?

JACE	You think just 'cause I'm stoned I don't know what's going on?
LENNY	When you were outside the house ... before you rang the bell...
JACE	I could've used earplugs. And I could smell your mom a mile away... I have to admit, I had you figured all wrong. I thought you were Miss Preppie Universe, but you're really just a different version of a screwed up mess like me.
LENNY	That's not true.
JACE	Maybe not for Leonore but it is for Tracy.
LENNY	You and I are completely different. My dad doesn't beat me up. I don't have to run away from home. My dad works really hard to keep things together and I do too. We have to keep working, we have to keep trying no matter how hard it gets because then... because then...
JACE	... then what?
LENNY	She'll get better. If we do it right maybe she'll get better.

***

Scene 27

from "Liars"

by Dennis Foon

1 female / 1 male

...OR DARE

Before you read this scene, read the previous one, TRUTH. In it, Jace reveals that he knows two secrets about his girlfriend, Lenny, and these truths bring them closer together. Once both Lenny and Jace acknowledge that their families don't live like 'normal families', Lenny is able open up a little to her new boyfriend.. This is where ...OR DARE begins at night, in the park, and two friends are getting down to some real, serious talk.

There is a kiss in this scene. Rehearse this **stage movement** just as you would your other cues. Position the taller actor **downstage** from the other actor, and then place his or her hands on the other's shoulders or, with permission, on either side of their face. (This is as much for balance and timing as romance .) Then use the **downstage** partner's head to **mask**, or obscure from the audience, the actual kiss, if you like. The audience won't know they missed a thing, especially if the **downstage** actor 'acts' the kiss by reacting (in a small way) with the shoulders.

Remember the most important part of the scene is the **sub-text** of the 'dare'. What does Jace dare Lenny to do, and what is her answer? And, why does a date that begins with such romance, end with such insults?

...Or Dare

LENNY	That's what real life is like, isn't it? I mean, normal families live like that, don't they?
JACE	What's normal? Listen to the news. It's just like our parents — fighting, lying, covering up. How can anybody be normal when the whole world's a stupid mess? I stopped believing in normal when I stopped believing in Santa Claus.
LENNY	... don't remind me of Christmas.
JACE	Your Christmases stink too, eh?
LENNY	I never know what to expect.
JACE	I do. Hell.
LENNY	Yeah, it's pretty bad.
JACE	How bad?
LENNY	Last year she passed out face down in the plum pudding.
JACE	My dad threw it at me.
LENNY	I bet he never knocked over the Christmas Tree.
JACE	No-but he puked on it.
LENNY	Really?
JACE	Just before we opened the presents.
LENNY	Gross.

JACE   And then he wanted me to try on my new sweater.

LENNY   ... I've never talked to anybody about this before. How come I can talk to you?

JACE   I don't know. I never talked to anybody about this stuff either.

LENNY   I feel kind of scared. Like I'm doing something wrong.

JACE   There's nothing wrong with talking.

LENNY   Unless you're in my house.

JACE   Same with mine.

LENNY   And at school, nobody talks.

JACE   Everybody talks-about nothing.

LENNY   You mean like boys and clothes and parties and school?

JACE   And cars and money and sex and drugs.

LENNY   I talk about that stuff, but that's not how I'm feeling inside. Inside I feel like I'm crazy.

JACE   Cause nobody talks about what's really going on.

LENNY   I'm always pretending everything's fine but I'm so scared. Sometimes I wonder why I'm alive. I feel completely useless.

JACE   There's nothing wrong with you. It's your parents who are useless. But I can see you. I can talk to you.

LENNY   ... I can talk to you too.

JACE	Yeah.
LENNY	Yeah.
	They kiss.
	I don't believe this.
JACE	What don't you believe?
LENNY	Everything. Meeting you. Being here. It seems too good to be true. Pinch me.
JACE	What?
LENNY	So I know it's real, it's not a dream.
JACE	You want me to pinch you ... okay.
	He does. LENNY yells in pain.
LENNY	Why'd you do it so hard!
JACE	Just following orders ... so is this a dream or reality?
LENNY	I'm not sure. What do you think? *(pinches JACE)*
JACE	OWW!! It's reality! Reality!
LENNY	... so do you want to make a deal?
JACE	What kinda deal?
LENNY	If you have a problem, you can talk to me. And if I have one, I'll talk to you.
JACE	Not like our parents, eh?
LENNY	We'll really listen. We'll really talk.
JACE	You got it.

LENNY	Deal?
JACE	Deal.

> *Pause. They start to kiss, but LENNY pulls away.*

LENNY	I better go now.
JACE	You can stay here if you want.
LENNY	I want to, but...
JACE	But what?
LENNY	I have to get home. I have to talk to them.
JACE	Why? Why go back there?
LENNY	I have to do something. Make them see.
JACE	It's a waste of time.
LENNY	I can help them change.
JACE	Forget it.
LENNY	I can't. Jace. I have to try... Are you going to be all right here?
JACE	I'll manage.
LENNY	What do you mean, you'll manage?
JACE	I'll manage.
LENNY	You mean, if I go, you'll get high?
JACE	Maybe.
LENNY	Yes or no?
JACE	What do you think?

LENNY	Maybe I'd better not go.
JACE	That's no reason to stay.
LENNY	Why? I want to help you.
JACE	I don't need that kind of help. I'm not your mother.
LENNY	I know that.
JACE	If I get high it's my business. If you want to stay here to help yourself, fine. But don't think it's gonna change me somehow. You can't change me anymore than you can change your Parents. Give it up.
LENNY	But I can't run away from it like you. And I won't stay high so I don't have to face it.
JACE	You just wanna be the perfect little daughter.
LENNY	You're the perfect little son.
JACE	What're you talking about?
LENNY	You're a chip off the old block.
JACE	No way! I'm not like him, I'll never be like him. Never.
LENNY	But you are. You just use different drugs, that's all.
JACE	I'm nothing like him. Nothing! You're the one who's gonna end up all teeth and furs and fancy clothes and drunk as a skunk in her five-bedroom house. Not me. I'm never going back.
LENNY	Jace, I have to go.
JACE	Good. Go on. Go save 'em, Supergirl.

LENNY   Goodnight.

JACE   Watch out for the Kryptonite.

                     LENNY exits. JACE reaches into his pack, pulls out a small bag.

                     Up, up and away.

                              * * *

Scene 28

from "Yellow on Thursdays"

by Sara Graefe

2 females / 1 male

EVERYBODY'S DIFFERENT

This is the second of Sara Graefe's three scene story about Katie (see Scene 8), a high school senior student who discovers a new part of her own sexuality when Mike comes between Katie and her best friend, Rebecca.

Since Katie finds it difficult to talk to Rebecca about her new feelings (the usual way writers let us know what a character is thinking), Sara Graefe uses some clever, playwriting devices to let us in on Katie's emotions, and to bring the audience closer to her than either Mike or Rebecca, making Katie the character we care most about.

The first of these is the short, single line in which Katie says "What if I'm real different?" The preceding stage direction, *"Katie, alone,"* tells us that this one-line **monologue** is really a tiny **soliloquy**, because no one hears Katie but the audience. It has the same *purpose*, at least as Hamlet's famous 'To be or not to be' speech, that is, to reveal a character's true emotions, ones they can trust to no one.

Rebecca's next line, even though it comes *before* the new **stage direction**, *"... in the school bathroom,"* is both a scary comment on Katie's "real different" line (did Rebecca hear me just then?), that would startle Katie, *and* the **transition** to the next scene in the washroom, where it is obvious that Rebecca is talking about her sister, not Katie.

So, the challenge in this scene is to get this clever **dramatic irony** across to the audience without stopping the scene to read the preceding paragraphs mid-performance! The trick is in the **timing** of the **transition**, an **exit** and **freeze** by

Rebecca and, if it can be managed, a smooth **light change** to establish the two **settings**. The following page repeats this **transition** with a longer **soliloquy**, another setting, and an "echo" - use your imagination!

Everybody's Different

REBECCA and KATIE in REBECCA's room.

KATIE   Hey, what's with all the new posters?

REBECCA   Like 'em?

KATIE   They're alright.

REBECCA   Mike's favourite bands.

KATIE   Mike, Mike, Mike. What about you?

REBECCA   What do you mean?

KATIE   C'mon, Becca, I thought you hated grunge!

REBECCA   Well, people are allowed to change their minds, you know.

KATIE   You're hilarious!

REBECCA   What?

KATIE   You totally bend over backwards to please a guy.

REBECCA   So?!

KATIE   Just an observation.

REBECCA   You're as bad as my sister. Ever since she started university, she's turned into this raving feminist who won't let me have fun—

KATIE   Hey, relax, would you? I guess you really like him, that's all.

REBECCA   Yeah. Big time.

KATIE   What's it like?

REBECCA What?

KATIE   You know, liking a guy.

REBECCA Really amazing ... you know.

KATIE   Do you feel anything?

REBECCA What?!

KATIE   Like when you're close...

REBECCA Well, yeah!

KATIE   What's it like'?

REBECCA Kinda like electricity — just like when you see a cute guy who really turns you on, only it's more intense, y'know?

KATIE   Yeah? Wow...

REBECCA Hey, stop worrying, you! Your time'll come.

KATIE   What if I don't feel anything?

REBECCA Don't worry, you will.

KATIE   What — what if I've never felt anything...

REBECCA Everybody's different...

KATIE, alone.

KATIE   What if I'm real different?

REBECCA You'd think she was a friggin' lesbian or something!

REBECCA and KATIE in the school bathroom.

KATIE What?

REBECCA My sister. She's been making me mental! Her ugly buzz cut and "I don't need a man in my life right now." and "You don't value yourself enough, Rebecca, you throw yourself away for any man who comes along." I mean she was just like me when she was in high school, except then it was OK and cool... But see, she doesn't want to see her baby sister to make the same mistakes she did. She learned the hard way.

KATE Oh please.

REBECCA Tell me about it.

Pause.

KATIE Do you think ... she is?

REBECCA What?

KATIE A lesbian.

REBECCA I don't know... God — can you imagine?

Katie, alone.

KATIE I try to picture Becca's sister kissing another woman. It doesn't really work, she keeps turning into my French teacher like in my dream and suddenly I'm feeling really crazy again... Crazy 'cause I can't get these pictures out of my head, Becca's sister and Mme. Dufresne and even Becca, Becca and the dimple in her cheek and her dancing eyes... Electricity, I can feel it, just like Becca was saying—

REBECCA　　　　　*(an echo)* God — can you imagine?

　　　　　　　　　REBECCA and MIKE entangled in front of the lockers.

MIKE　　　　　　What's with her, anyways?

REBECCA　　　　What do you mean?

MIKE　　　　　　She's always hanging around.

REBECCA　　　　She's my best friend.

MIKE　　　　　　I didn't realize going out with you was a package deal.

REBECCA　　　　What's that supposed to mean?

MIKE　　　　　　I mean, I like her and everything, but does she have to be around all the time—

　　　　　　　　　KATIE enters.

KATIE　　　　　　Hey, guys.

REBECCA　　　　Hi.

　　　　　　　　　MIKE shoots REBECCA a look. KATIE catches it.

KATIE　　　　　　What's up?

REBECCA　　　　Nothing.

KATIE　　　　　　*(to MIKE)* How's it going?

MIKE　　　　　　Alright.

　　　　　　　　　Awkward pause.

REBECCA　　　　So.

KATIE	What's new?
REBECCA	Not much. You?
KATIE	Stressed. We have way too much work this year. I just spent hours on that stupid French assignment—
MIKE	Oh shoot.
KATIE	You didn't do it?
MIKE	When, are you kidding? She's going to burn me, man!
KATIE	You'll probably get out of it. She likes you 'cause you're from Montreal.
MIKE	What?
KATIE	She does, haven't you noticed?
MIKE	Yeah, well, she likes you 'cause you're a brown-noser.
KATIE	Thanks! Am not!
MIKE	You're her little pet.
KATIE	No way!
MIKE	You're always so intense in class. You should see her—
KATIE	OK, so maybe I like French—
REBECCA	She's just practicing for when that French lover comes along.
MIKE	What?!
KATIE & REBECCA	"French lovers are supposed to be the best, you know!"

They laugh, making their Saliva Sisters sign. MIKE is uncomfortable.

MIKE — I'll leave you two to it.

REBECCA — Hey, where you going?

KATIE — Look, it's OK, I'll go—

REBECCA — Katie.

KATIE — I mean, if I'm butting in—

REBECCA — You're not—

MIKE — Look, I'm outta here.

He leaves.

REBECCA — Mike!

KATIE — Sorry.

REBECCA — It's not your fault.

KATIE — I don't think he likes me.

REBECCA — He likes you fine.

KATIE — But I'm just the third wheel, right?

REBECCA — No.

KATIE — It's OK, I can take a hint.

REBECCA — Well—

KATIE — Well?

REBECCA — Sort of. Yeah.

Pause.

KATIE — Well, great.

REBECCA	Hey, you asked.
KATIE	So I'd rather know. We've always been honest with each other.
REBECCA	Katie, it's just — it gets so complicated with a guy in the picture. It's like — I have this whole new understanding of the world and — I mean, it'd be easier if you found a guy too.
KATIE	I don't know...
REBECCA	We could double date and stuff. It'd be so fun! Kinda like old times.
KATIE	With a twist.
REBECCA	Yeah, with a twist!
KATIE	Sounds kinda fun.
REBECCA	It'd be a blast!
KATIE	So hey, what do you say — I'll just have to go to the dance on Friday and pick up some hot guys!
REBECCA	Hey, right on!
KATIE	Like — what do you think of Rob Arthurs? He's kind of cute, isn't he?
REBECCA	He's a regular babefest!
KATIE	Well hey — looks like I'm all set!
REBECCA	GO GIRL!!!

They squeal and make their Saliva Sisters sign.

———

MIKE and REBECCA in the hall.

MIKE	Since when is she coming to the dance with us?
REBECCA	Since yesterday.
MIKE	Well thanks for telling me
REBECCA	I didn't think you'd mind.
MIKE	I don't get it — who am I dating here? Rebecca, or the Blood Sister Twins?
REBECCA	That's Saliva Sisters.
MIKE	Whatever. I've been hearing stuff, you know.
REBECCA	What kind of stuff.?
MIKE	'Bout you and her.
REBECCA	Like what?
MIKE	Like how you two are always hanging out together. Like you're joined at the hip.
REBECCA	Yeah, and?
MIKE	And until this year, you never dated guys...
REBECCA	So?
MIKE	Jay Crandall said you were a bunch of lezzies. I wanted to punch him right there—
REBECCA	What? Jay Crandall is full of crap, you know that! I can't believe you even listened to that jerk! You didn't believe him, did you?
MIKE	Well ... I don't know...
REBECCA	Mike, Katie's my best friend! I never — we never — I don't believe this! Are you jealous of Katie?!

MIKE	Like I said, I've been hearing stuff...
REBECCA	Well, like, use your brain!
MIKE	Look, I'm sorry. What do you want? I'm new 'round here...
REBECCA	Don't you trust me?

    Pause.

***

Scene 29

"Buster"

by R.L. Goodwin

1 female / 1 male

Darleen and Jake appear to be just another travelling young couple spending the night in a motel. He's interested in romance; she wants to bring 'Buster' in from the car so he won't get cold. But, Buster turns out to be something much more than the family dog. And, Darleen, much more than either we, or Jake, bargained for.

Without giving too much away, you will need a couple of **technical effects** to make this scene 'work'. First, the body of Buster — there is no need to even let the audience see Buster's face, even for the last line, if Darleen and Buster are positioned well on the stage. Since Jake has to carry Buster, a blanket stuffed to body size would be far easier to work with than a real person. (Besides, you don't want someone playing the body to destroy the wonderful tension of your scene with a silly move or gesture). The gun should be simply a plastic one, timed with a great **sound effect**. Again, effective **blocking** is the best tool. Let Jake carry 'the body' to **downstage centre**, while Darleen stands, gun drawn, behind him. After he lowers the body, stands and turns **upstage** to face her, he effectively **masks** the gun. Four shots (and four great **reactions** from Jake) and he slumps to the stage, leaving the audience a clear **sight line** of our serial killer, gun slowly lowering.

Ragna Goodwin has written a script remarkably full of surprises for its short length. And, she's created in Darleen one of those fabulous, ultra-cool ladies from the old murder movies, brimming with self-confidence and deadly force — a powerful and fun role to play.

Buster

The curtain opens to a cheap motel room on a rainy night. A couple in their mid-twenties enter. The man is well groomed, wearing a business suit and wire-framed glasses. The woman is in a long, floral dress with her hair pulled back. Each are carrying an overnight bag, laughing and shaking off rain.

JAKE
(*tosses his bag on the bed, loosens his tie, and surveys room*) Well, what did I tell you? Nothing too good for you, love.

DARLEEN
(*lays her bag next to his*) Oh, don't be silly. It's fine. We're only here to sleep.

JAKE
(*comes around behind her and encircles his arms around her waist*) Not just to sleep, surely.

DARLEEN
(*turning around, saying seductively*) Well, you just may be in luck. (*voice picks up*) There appears to be a TV, too. (*kissing him lightly on the cheek*) And don't call me Shirley.

JAKE moans and flops down on the bed in defeat.

DARLEEN
(*begins to open one of the bags then pauses, and turns to JAKE looking worried*) Angel?

JAKE
Huummmh?

DARLEEN
Are you sure Buster will be all right out in the car all night?

JAKE
(*sitting up and taking off his jacket*) He'll be fine, Hon.

DARLEEN
But it's raining ...

JAKE	Not in the car.
DARLEEN	*(starts to say something, but stops, dismissive, and smiles)* You must be tired from that long drive.
JAKE	*(pulling her onto his lap)* A little.
DARLEEN	Would you like me to run you a nice hot bath?
JAKE	Well, now; that all depends. Will you be joining me?
DARLEEN	But I'm not dirty...
JAKE	It's never too late to change ...
DARLEEN	*(smiling absently, running her fingers through his hair)* You don't think it's too cold do you?
JAKE	To be dirty?
DARLEEN	No silly. For Buster.
JAKE	*(exhaling annoyed)* Honey, we agreed...
DARLEEN	It isn't too cold, is it?
JAKE	No, Honey. But just in case I left a blanket for him to curl up in. All right? *(he begins to massage her shoulders)*
DARLEEN	*(reaching up holding his hands still)* Can't we just sneak him in here with us?
JAKE	*(firmly, standing her up, and moving away)* No. If the manager catches on, all three of us will be spending the night out in the car ... *(he turns back to her, his voice softening)* Besides, I have plans for us that do not involve a captive audience.

> JAKE pulls *her close* to *him and slowly undoes her hair, letting it fall around her shoulders.* DARLEEN *closes her eyes and smiles dreamily.*

DARLEEN We could lock him in the bathroom...

JAKE *(jerking away)* Oh, for the love of... You're the one who insisted we bring him along in the first place! If you knew you were going to be so concerned the entire trip, why didn't we just leave him?!

DARLEEN I'm sorry, I just don't think—

JAKE No kidding you just don't think! This is our time together now. A clean start, remember? I won't have you ruining it up by fawning over Buster all night.

DARLEEN *(very calmly and very clearly)* I want this time together with you, too. But I just can't. Not with him out there. I want to be with you completely. But I won't be able to do that if my mind keeps wandering ... if I can't stop thinking about him. Alone, cold...

JAKE All right! Fine. I'll go out and get him. But good old Buster stays locked in the bathroom. Got it?

DARLEEN *(sighs with relief)* Deal.

> JAKE *leaves, slamming the door.* DARLEEN *walks over to the mirror on the dresser and fluffs out her hair. She pauses thoughtfully, gently pinches her cheeks, runs her tongue over her lips and undoes the first two buttons on her dress. She walks back over to the bed and reaches into one of the bags and pulls out a Smith & Wesson 9mm. She unlatches the safety and stands with her back to the door and her finger on the trigger.*

We hear the door open, and JAKE enters, stumbling a little, huffing and grunting mildly, half carrying and half dragging something heavy and awkward. There is a final thud, as he drops something to the floor.

JAKE	There. Happy now? All contented?

DARLEEN	*(slowly smiling)* Quite.

She spins around and aims the gun at JAKE. Just as his face registers what's happening she shoots him in the chest four times. He slams back against the door and falls dead to the ground.

DARLEEN	*(straightening her shoulders and tossing her hair back)* A clean start, Angel.

She tosses the gun onto the bed and walks over to where JAKE had dropped Buster. Lying on the ground, bound and gagged, we see the body of a young man, early twenties, who has apparently been shot in the chest. Darleen drops down next to the body and cradles the head in her lap. She strokes his hair back and kisses him on the forehead, crying.

DARLEEN	It's over now, Sweetheart. It's just us. From now on ... it's just us ... just us ...

Fade to black.

* * *

Scene 30

"Don't Call Me That"

by Alicia Payne

1 female / 2 males

Shane is upset because Steven called her a name she didn't like; Steven didn't expect the kind of reaction he got, and regrets his actions ... 411 to the rescue to restore the peace in his own way.

Note the first stage direction "Shane bursts onto the scene". This doesn't mean walk. This is as energized an opening, and ending for that matter, as you will find in any scene in the book. Fast action and anger demand **quick line cues** which gives a **fast pace**. That fact alone earns this apparently straightforward scene a place in this section. Be warned: know your lines cold. By the way, "Stop, in the Name of Love" is a Sixties song by The Supremes. Ask your teacher to sing a few bars to get the melody.

Don't Call Me That

Characters SHANE, 411, STEVEN — all three are students. The setting is a school.

SHANE bursts onto the scene, angry, looking for STEVEN. 411 follows her, out of breath.

SHANE   Come out, come out, wherever you are. Don't worry, I won't hurt you ... too badly.

411   Maybe if you stopped yelling you could sneak up on him.

SHANE   Get outta my face.

411   He can hear you coming a mile away.

SHANE   Check over there.

411   If you were looking for me, like I'd wait for you.

SHANE   Just check.

SHANE and 411 exit. STEVEN enters.

STEVEN   Man, oh man. I'm dead. That's it. I'm dead. They're gonna lynch me. Da— darn it. A word. One word stood between me and death and wouldn't you know, I used it. Don't look at me like that. Everybody else was saying it. I meant it in a good way. All I said was— *(he's interrupted by the sound of 411's voice)*

411   *(offstage)* Nobody here but us chickens. *(clucking)*

STEVEN   Gotta jet!

411 enters as STEVEN exits. They almost bump into each other.

411 Whoah! Relax, she's over there somewhere. Oh, man, you're history. What'd you say?

STEVEN Nothing.

411 You had to say something.

STEVEN I said something but it was nothing.

SHANE *(enters) Make* me run and you're dust.

411 You can't run forever. She will find you. *(megaphone voice)* We've got you cornered. Give yourself up and you won't get hurt.

STEVEN Shane. Words. What are they? They don't mean anything. Okay, they mean something but when I use them I don't mean anything by them. You know what I mean?

SHANE No, but I guarantee you'll know what I mean.

STEVEN Look, I'm sorry. I didn't mean anything by it.

SHANE Then why'd you call me that?

411 Call you what?

STEVEN I called you that but that's not what I meant by that.

SHANE What'd you mean then?

STEVEN Ahhh, ahhh ....

411 We're waiting. What'd he call you?

SHANE Any time now.

411 What'd you call her?

STEVEN   I've heard other people call you that.

SHANE   Only certain people.

STEVEN   So I'm not part of the group? Is that what you're saying? I've even heard you say that.

SHANE   You're not like me so you can't call me that.

STEVEN   Well, if its so bad, why do you call each other that?

SHANE   Because.

411   Each other who? Call each other what?

STEVEN   *(to 411)* Will you just...*(turning to SHANE)* I'm sorry. What now?

SHANE   I break your face.

411   You shouldn't've called her that.

STEVEN   Called her what?

411   You know.

STEVEN   You're gonna break my face just because I called you that?

SHANE   Among other things. Should I teach you a lesson and then break your face? Or should I break your face and then teach you a lesson?

411   *(singing)* Ooooooh, you're gonna get. Ooooh, are you ever gonna get it.

STEVEN   She's too much. What do you think? All I said was—

SHANE   Hey! Don't say it again.

STEVEN   Then how's he supposed to know if you're overreacting or not?

SHANE   Who cares what he thinks? I'm the one who was insulted.

STEVEN   I didn't insult you ... on purpose. Sensitive or what?

SHANE   I'll "or what" you in a minute.

411   *(singing)* STOP, in the name of love, before you break his face.
Think it over.
Yeah, think it 0h-oh-ver.
Hmmmmm.
(making referee signals) Time out! Friends, Romans, country men ... people. Country people and fellow scholars. I don't know what you called her and I really want to know but, right now, it's not important. All I know is that one of my good friends wants to pulverize the other one and that's not good. No, not good at all. Lucky for you, however, I can solve your problem for a small fee. Payable later. Or not payable at all. I'm flexible. Now, let me see. You are the insulter and you are the insultee.

SHANE   And you're gonna be dead in a minute.

411   Be not too hasty with thy fist, good woman. I'm doing this for you.

SHANE   I can take care of myself, thanks.

411   Well then., I'm doing this for Steven. Just take a deep breath and hang on a second, Okay? Whatever he called you, maybe he wasn't smart enough to know any better.

STEVEN   Very funny.

411   I will facilitate your peace treaty. Mighty Mediator at your service. You cool with that?

SHANE	For now.
STEVEN	And?
411	And what?
STEVEN	Yeah and what?
411	We communicate and your life will be spared. The insultee will tell the insulter what they think.
SHANE	Got that right.
STEVEN	And what if people can't agree on who's the insulter and the insultee? I don't like being called the insulter and she said some pretty nasty things to me even though I don't know what was wrong with what I said.
SHANE	You should know
STEVEN	But I don't.
SHANE	Let me explain.
411	Hold up! Hold up. I think this is going pretty well. You're talking aren't you? Okay, the person who's the hottest goes first.
SHANE	Hmm! There is no contest.
411	I mean, the person who is hottest under the collar, you know? The most upset.
SHANE	Still no contest.
STEVEN	Oh yeah? And what if you can't decide who's the hottest? I'm pretty upset now too, you know.
411	How did you know there was a problem between you two?

STEVEN	She threw her shoe at my head and called me ... some stuff. Okay, she goes first.
411	"She" has a name, which leads me to rule number one. Rule number one: No, I mean, NO name calling. Rule number two: One speaks, the other listens, 'cause everyone gets a chance to flap at the gums. Okay, here's how we do it. You say, Steven, when you BLANK — fill in the blank — I feel BLANK and I wish you would BLANK because BLANK. Don't forget to fill in the blanks.
SHANE	Big Mouth—
411	Houston, we've got a problem. No name-calling. Just tell him what he did and how it made you feel. Action.
SHANE	Steven, when you called me that, I felt like punching you out and—
411	Punching someone out is not a feeling. You felt like doing it but that's not how you felt. Were you happy when he called you whatever he call you? Embarrassed? Sad? Angry maybe?
SHANE	Maybe if you stopped interrupting I could tell him.
411	I'm not interrupting. I'm facilitating.
STEVEN	Why me?
	Each time SHANE attempts to speak. 411 cuts in.
411	Continue. *(pause)* You're doin' great. *(pause)* Take your time. I'll shut up now.
SHANE	Steven, when you called me that, I was mad and I wish you would never, I mean, never, ever, ever, ever, ever, even if your

	grandmother asks you to, ever, ever call me that again. Ever. And apologize for real.
411	Because...
SHANE	Because I'd have to punch you out. And stop being your friend.
SHANE	Good' Not that you'd punch him out but you filled in all the blanks.
411	Okay, Steven. You get to respond. Isn't this fun?
STEVEN	Shane, if I knew you would be so upset I would never have called you that. I still don't understand why you got so mad but that's cool. All I know is I upset you, I didn't mean to and I'm sorry. Really. You down with that?
SHANE	Yeah, I'm cool.
411	*(sighs)* That's beautiful. *(faking tears)* I'm touched.
STEVEN	I guess you got how 411 gets if someone calls him Byron.
	411 freezes.
SHANE	Byron?
411	*(his hand begins to tremble slightly)* Don't call me that.
STEVEN	Yeah. Didn't you know Byron was his real name?
411	*(the trembling increases)* Don't call me that.
STEVEN	He just loses it.
SHANE	Why?

> *411 clasps his hands behind him and starts slowly pacing back and forth.*

STEVEN — I don't know. Maybe something happened when he was younger or something.

SHANE — Why can't we call you Byron? If that's your real name you should be proud of it. Too bad for anyone else.

411 — *(he freezes again)* Don't anybody ever call me that.

STEVEN — Uh-oh. He's gonna erupt.

411 — I hate that.

STEVEN — Let's jet.

SHANE — We haven't thanked him yet.

STEVEN — Let's thank him later.

411 — *(pacing back and forth)* Don't call me that. Don't call me that. Don't, don't, don't call me that. I really hate that. I mean, I really, really hate that. My mother doesn't even call me that. So just DON'T CALL ME THAT!.

SHANE — Sorry, Bye— Oops.

STEVEN — Run.

411 — ARGHHHHHHHH!!!!!

SHANE — *(laughing)* Oh Mighty Mediator, we need you.

> *411 chases SHANE and STEVEN off stage.*

* * *

Scene 31

from "Zastrozzi, The Master of Discipline"

by George F. Walker

2 males

THE MASTER CRIMINAL

"Zastrozzi, The Master of Discipline", is the full title from which this selection is taken. It is the original **comedy noir** of Canadian theatre, first produced in Toronto in 1977. In the two decades that followed, George F. Walker was (and still is) one of a handful of English Canadian playwrights who can sell out the house with their name alone.

Zastrozzi, as you will read, is "the master criminal" of all Europe, seeking revenge on an artist known as Verezzi, who is protected by Victor, the most reasonable man in the play. Because this is **comedy noir** style (explained in the introduction to Scene 17), Zastrozzi is larger than life; more evil, more dangerous, more powerful — and less moral — than any character we have seen so far. He is the school-yard bully times ten, with a very bad attitude and a very sharp sword. But, for the actor, characters don't come any nicer.

Victor must be played in an exaggerated fashion as well. You would think that, because he is defenseless, he wouldn't say anything to anger Zastrozzi, and if he did unintentionally upset him, leave the room at the first chance. But, even when Zastrozzi has his sword to Victor's throat, he remains calm. Victor has a power of his own; one you must discover and show in his **reactions** to Zastrozzi.

Don't use sharp weapons in this scene! You don't even need a sword; use a rubber dagger. Every good actor can draw the audience's **focus** from the prop to the danger in his **voice** and **movements**, a much more entertaining place for evil than a mere sword. Of course, the final flourish with his weapon must be a well-rehearsed and impressive display.

The Master Criminal

> *The sky is rumbling again. ZASTROZZI is drunk. He is it the doorway of his bed chamber. he drinks the last of the wine in his flask and throws it on the floor.*

ZASTROZZI Where is my wine? I called for that wine an hour ago. I warn you it is in your best interest to keep me drunk. I am at my mellowest when drunk. Innkeeper?

A VOICE Coming, sir.

> *ZASTROZZI grunts. Goes and sits in a chair near the bed. Picks up a book. Reads. Grunts. Grunts louder. Throws the book across the room.*

ZASTROZZI Liar! *(standing, pacing)* They're all liars. Why do I read books? What is this new age of optimism they're all talking about? It's a lie sponsored by the church and the government to give people false hope. The people. I care less about the people than I do about the church or the government. Then what do you care about sin. I care that I should not ask myself questions like that. I care to be dumb, and without care. I care that I should not ask myself questions like that ever again.

> *He sits. Pause.*

Sad.

> *He stands.*

Wine!.

He sits.

Sad.

VICTOR enters with the wine.

ZASTROZZI   Who are you?

VICTOR   I own this inn.

ZASTROZZI   No. I've met the owner.

VICTOR   The former owner. I won it from him in a card game last night.

ZASTROZZI   Congratulations. Put the wine down and get out.

VICTOR puts the wine down.

VICTOR   You are the Great Zastrozzi, aren't you?

ZASTROZZI   I *am a* lodger in your inn.

VICTOR   Are you ashamed of being Zastrozzi?

ZASTROZZI   If you were to die in the near future would many people attend your funeral?

VICTOR   No.

ZASTROZZI   Then save yourself the embarrassment. Get out.

VICTOR   I heard that Zastrozzi once passed through Paris like a plague. Leaving the aristocracy nearly bankrupt, their daughters all defiled and diseased, the police in chaos and the museums ransacked. And all because, it is said, he took a dislike to the popular French taste in art.

ZASTROZZI   A slight exaggeration. He took a dislike to a certain aristocratic artist who happened to have a very willing daughter and one painting in one museum.

VICTOR   And did Zastrozzi kill the artist, rape his daughter and destroy the painting?

ZASTROZZI   The daughter was not touched. She had syphilis. Probably given to her by the father. The painting was not worth destroying. It was just removed from the illustrious company it had no right to be with.

He takes a drink.

VICTOR   But the artist was killed.

ZASTROZZI   Yes. Certainly.

VICTOR   Why?

ZASTROZZI   To prove that even artists must answer to somebody.

VICTOR   And what has Zastrozzi come to this obscure place to prove?

ZASTROZZI   Zastrozzi is starting some new endeavour. He is going to murder only inn-keepers for a year.

VICTOR   I am not afraid of you.

ZASTROZZI   Then you are stupid. *(pause)* And you are not an innkeeper.

VICTOR   They say that all Europe has no more cause to fear Zastrozzi. They say that for three years he has been single-minded in a search for revenge on one man and that all the rest of Europe has been untouched.

ZASTROZZI   They think and say only what Zastrozzi wants them to think and say.

VICTOR   They also say that any man can cross him, that any woman can use him. Because the master criminal, the Great Zastrozzi, is in a trance.

ZASTROZZI   Ah. But then there are trances ... *(drawing his sword and doing four or five amazing things with it.)* ... and there are trances.

He puts the sword to VICTOR's throat.

Now, who are you?

***

Scene 32

from "New Canadian Kid"

by Dennis Foon

2 characters

Lo, Nicknick

One of the biggest problems facing kids new to Canada is of course, mastering Canadian English. If you wanted to write a play about this, and other, issues facing new immigrants you wouldn't have a very realistic play unless it was in two languages.

Dennis Foon's simple, elegant - and comic - solution to this problem is to use **gibberish**, a made up language used most often in **improv**. A lesser playwright would have had the immigrant kid speak in **gibberish**; Dennis Foon chose to have the Canadian kids use **gibberish** and the immigrant, Nick, speak in plain English. This puts the audience in the shoes of the immigrant. Brilliant.

Now, to speak **gibberish** in **improv**, because you have to make it up as you go, requires a great deal of practice. "New Canadian Kid" has scripted the **gibberish** just as if they were lines. **Memorize** them as you would any lines, because they contain jokes and puns necessary to the scene.

A note on character. Dennis Foon writes that Nick is a 'Homelander':

"Homelanders should look alien to the Canadians and to the audience, but their costumes (various shades of green) should not be identifiable to any specific country."

By making Nick a Homelander , the playwright creates a play about *all* immigrants, not just the current group. And in Canada, unless you are a member of this country's original immigrant group, the Amerindians, *your* family at some time in the past has experienced what Nick is going through now.

In this scene, Nick has just had his first day at the new school and it's been a disaster. His favourite possession was broken, he got in a fight, and he was called a "Sgak", **gibberish** for a racial slur, by Mug, a Canadian kid. In an effort to make up, Mug's friend, Mench, has brought over some sports stuff and intends to show Nick how to play some Canadian games. Mench can be played by either gender, as can Nick. It is very **physical** scene too - stay moving throughout, especially in the opening pantomime. Most of all, read it *aloud* first time, that way you'll hear the humour. Hast joksa [have fun]!

Lo, Nicknick

MENCH enters with a bag of sports equipment. NICK turns away, ignoring her.

MENCH   Lo, Nicknick. Sue vancha planch? [Hi, Nick. Do you want to play?]

She notices that his back is turned from her and that he is looking up. She goes over to him and tries to see what he is looking at.

Kel gander shtat? Kel Matso? Nicknick? [What are you looking at? What's the matter? Nick?]

She goes back to her sports bag, going through some of the things inside.

Ee brognay gorbso sportso eekwippo. Gander. Ein, doos, tweet .... [I brought gobs of sports equipment. Look. One, two, three ...]

NICK continues to ignore her.

(*in frustration*) Sue nax vancha planch, sue nax vancha planch. [Well, if you don't want to play, you don't want to play.]

She gives up and sneaks behind NICK.

NICK turns around and doesn't see her. Thinking MENCH has left, NICK goes to her sports bag. MENCH shadows him.

He looks inside the bag, takes out a baseball. As he takes it out he notices that MENCH is hiding behind him.

He stands up and walks in intricate circles, making MENCH struggle not to be seen.

He tosses the ball back and forth, making her run frantically as she tries to keep up with him and not be seen.

Finally he throws the ball behind him and MENCH inadvertently catches it, revealing herself. NICK looks at her.

They both laugh.

MENCH   Lo, Nicknick. [Hi, Nick.]

NICK   Lo, Menchamencha. [Hi, Menchamencha.]

MENCH   Nax. [No.] *(holding up* one finger) Mencha.

NICK   Nax. [No.] *(holding up* one finger) Nick.

MENCH   Nick?

NICK   Nick.

MENCH   *(hitting herself on the head)* Ohhh, yo.

NICK   Yo.

MENCH   *(handing NICK the glove)* Ee bee gerse glob glubber, Nick. [This is a baseball mitt, Nick.]

NICK   Gerse glob glibber.

MENCH   Bay perfecto! Nama .... [That's perfect! Nama...]

MENCH throws the ball. NICK catches it barehanded.

MENCH   Nax. Sue usta gerse glob grubber por kitz da gerseglob. [No. You use the baseball mitt to catch the baseball.]

NICK   I understand ....

MENCH notices that NICK hasn't even put the mitt on.

MENCH Nax, dos finger eight donk inksta gerse glob grubber. Cor cheesy. [No, your fingers go inside the glove. Like this.]

NICK Cor cheesy? [Like this?]

MENCH Yo. [Yes.]

MENCH throws the ball again. This time, NICK tries to use the mitt to hit the ball and sends it flying.

Nax, nax, sue usta gerse glob glibber por kitz da gerseglob. Nax shlam shtat. [No, no, you use the baseball mitt for catching the ball. Not hitting it.]

She demonstrates.

NICK I understand.

MENCH Ay? [Eh?]

NICK Oh. Yo, yo! [Yes, yes!]

MENCH Sue-she. [Okay.]

MENCH throws NICK a popfly. NICK catches it.

Kwee-sin-art! [Excellent!]

NICK Yo! [Yeah!]

MENCH Kitz! [Catch!]

NICK Bliss-tex! [Alright!] *(to audience)* So I started to make friends. I learned how to catch popshees ...
 He catches a fly ball.

>   ... and throw gutter globs ...
>
>   *He throws MENCH a ground ball.*
>
>   ... and how to put someone out at first ....
>
>   *He catches the ball and tags out an imaginary runner.*

MENCH   Sewer rat! [You're out!]

NICK   And I learned how to play shlamshtick.

>   *MENCH hands NICK a hockey stick and they both pretend to skate, passing the invisible puck back and forth.*

MENCH   Nama! [Now!]

>   *She passes to NICK.*

NICK   Spinarama! [Turn around!]

>   *NICK shoots.*

>   Chay chost! Chay shlamit! Chay scoro! [He shoots! He scores!] Yo! Ee bee Grain Wetsky! [Yeah! It's Wayne Gretzky!]
>
>   *They slap hands triumphantly, then hold hands in pain.*

NICK   (to audience) And I learned to eat good Canadian foods, like—

>   *MENCH throws a basketball to NICK.*

MENCH   Baykee Lassee!

NICK   (catching the ball) Hot dogs! (he throws it back)

MENCH   Grosta Mack! (throws it to NICK)

NICK	Hamburgers! *(throws it back)*
MENCH	Greesee spudniks! *(throws to NICK)*
NICK	French fries! *(throws it back)*
MENCH	Chubbee blubber! *(throws to NICK)*
NICK	Double Bubble! *(throws it back)*
MENCH	Tweet shtay mik freezee moomoo mik cheetah chumps mik bakee sludge mik wing wong mik snikker giggle la tip top.
	She throws to NICK.
NICK	Three scoops of ice cream with bananas, hot fudge, peanuts, sprinkles ...
	He throws the ball to MENCH.
	... and a giant Snickers bar on top.
	MENCH throws the ball back, it hits him in the stomach. NICK groans.
NICK	And stomach aches ... and I got a Nickeejocko.
	MENCH helps him put on a nylon jacket that has an adapted 'Nike' logo.
NICK	I was doing pretty good. And my English? I could speak ...
MENCH	Sue-she. [So-so.]

* * *

Scene 33

from "Billy Bishop Goes to War"

by John Gray and Eric Peterson

2 males

FIGHTER PILOT

    John Gray is a Canadian who writes successful musicals — "18 Wheels" and "Rock and Roll". "Billy Bishop Goes To War" took him and his partner, stage and TV actor, Eric Peterson (of "Street Legal" fame), to Broadway in 1980. They wrote *and* performed the play from which the following scene is taken; John Gray played the piano and Eric Peterson played all the characters - even in the dialogues!

    This scene doesn't require any singing - or playing two characters at once. You should **double** however. The actor playing Billy Bishop stays as Billy, the partner plays first the drunken Officer, and then 'stiff upper-lip' (and sober) Sir Hugh. (If you really want to add an interesting layer, use a Cockney **dialect** with the Officer, and an upper-class British one for Sir Hugh.)

    Billy Bishop, of course, was Canada's most famous hero from World War One. He shot down 72 enemy planes by 1918, a record surpassed only by the famous Red Baron, Manfred Von Richthofen. But Bishop survived the war (another Canadian, Roy Brown, killed the Red Baron) becoming honorary Air Marshall of the RCAF in World War Two.

    Here, Bishop has just arrived on the field of battle as a Cavalry Officer; a muddy, grim assignment he hates. One night, on leave in England, he starts a conversation in a pub with a British Officer - and the audience learns how Billy Bishop got his wings..

Find some **period music** (a little research) to accompany the scene, a fast **costume** change for the Officer/Sir Hugh, and if you need to brush up on **direct address**, see the intro. to Scene 2.

Fighter Pilot

> *The piano continues with a popular dance tune of the period. BISHOP's reverie is interrupted by a Cockney OFFICER, who is also drunk and slightly mad.*

OFFICER You don't fancy the Cavalry then, eh?

BISHOP What?!

OFFICER I say, you don't fancy the Cavalry then, eh? It's going to be worse at the front, mate. There, you got blokes shooting at you, right? ... with machine guns. *imitating a machine-gun)* DakDakDakDakakaka. Har, har, har. It's a bloody shooting gallery. They still think they're fighting the Boer War! Cavalry charges against machine guns. DakDakDakak. Har, bar! It's a bloody shooting gallery with you in the middle of it, mate.

BISHOP This is awful. Something's got to be done. Jeez, I was a casualty in training.

OFFICER Take a word of advice from me, mate. The only way out is up.

BISHOP Up?

OFFICER Up. Join the Royal Flying Corps. I did. I used to be in the Cavalry, but I joined the R.F.C. I like it. It's good clean work. Mind you, the bleeding machines barely stay in the air and the life expectancy of the new lads is about eleven days. But I like it. It's good clean work.

BISHOP   Just a minute. How can I get into the Royal Flying Corps? I'm a Canadian. I'm cannon fodder. You practically have to own your own plane to get into the R. F. C.

OFFICER *Au contraire*, mate. *Au contraire.* The upper classes are depressed by the present statistics, so they, aren't joining with their usual alacrity. Now, anyone who wants to can get blown out of the air. Even Canadians.

BISHOP   Well, what do I have to do?

OFFICER You go down to see them at the War Office, daft bunch of twits, but they're alright. Now ... you act real eager, see? Like you want to be a pilot. You crave the excitement, any old rubbish like that. Then, they're not going to know what to ask, because they don't know a bleeding thing about it. So, they'll ask you whatever comes into their heads, which isn't much, then they'll say you can't be a pilot, you've got to be an observer.

BISHOP   What's an observer?

OFFICER He's the fellow who goes along for the ride, You know? Looks about.

BISHOP   Ohhh ....

OFFICER So, you act real disappointed, like your Mum wanted you to be a pilot, and then, you get your transfer ...

BISHOP   Just a minute. So, I'm an observer. I'm the fellow that goes along for the ride, looks about. So what? How do I get to be a pilot?

OFFICER I don't know. Sooner or later, you just get to be a pilot. Plenty of vacancies these days. Check the casualty lists, wait for a bad one.

You've got to go in by the back door, you know what I mean? Nobody gets to be a pilot right away, for Christ's sake. Especially not bleeding Canadians!

BISHOP *(to the audience)* Did you ever trust your future to a drunken conversation in *a bar*? Two days later, I went down to see them at the War Office.

The PIANO PLAYER plays some going-to-war music. In the following scene, SIR HUGH CECIL interviews BISHOP at the War Office. He is getting on in years and the new technology of warfare has confused him deeply.

SIR HUGH So ... you wish to transfer to the Royal Flying Corps? Am I right? Am I correct?

BISHOP Yes, sir. I want to become a fighter pilot, sir. It's what my mother always wanted, sir.

SIR HUGH Oh ... I see. Well, the situation is this, Bishop. We need good men in the R.F.C. but they must have the correct ... er ... qualifications. Now, while the War Office has not yet ascertained what qualifications are indeed necessary to fly an ... er ... aeroplane, we must see to it that all candidates possess the necessary qualifications, should the War Office ever decide what those qualifications are. Do you understand, Bishop?

BISHOP Perfectly, Sir.

SIR HUGH That's very good. Jolly good. More than I can say. Well, shall we begin then?

BISHOP Ready when you are, Sir.

SIR HUGH	That's good, shows keenness, you see... And good luck, Bishop. *(to himself)* What on earth shall I ask him? *(There is a long pause while he collects his thoughts.)* Do you ski?
BISHOP	Ski, sir?
SIR HUGH	Yes ... do you ski?
BISHOP	*(to the audience)* Here was an Englishman asking *a Canadian* whether or not he skied. Now, if the Canadian said he didn't ski, the Englishman might find that somewhat suspicious. *(to SIR HUGH)* Ski? Yes, Sir. *(to the audience)* Never skied in my life.
SIR HUGH	Fine, well done . . . thought you might. *(pause)* Do you ride a horse?
BISHOP	I'm an officer in the Cavalry, Sir.
SIR HUGH	Doesn't necessarily follow, but we'll put down that you ride, shall we? *(pause)* What about sports, Bishop? Run, jump, throw the ball? Play the game, eh? What?
BISHOP	Sports, sir? All sports.
SIR HUGH	I see. Well done, Bishop. I'm most impressed.
BISHOP	Does this mean I can become a fighter pilot, sir?
SIR HUGH	Who knows, Bishop? Who knows? All full up with fighter pilots at the moment, I'm afraid. Take six months, a year to get in. Terribly sorry. Nothing I can do, old man.
BISHOP	I see, sir.

SIR HUGH   However! We have an immediate need for observers. You know, the fellow who goes along for the ride, looks about. What do you say, Bishop?

BISHOP   *(to the audience)* I thought about it. I wanted to be a pilot. I couldn't. So, in the fall of 1915, I joined the Twenty-First Squadron as an observer. That's what they were using planes for at that time. Observation. You could take pictures of enemy troop formations, direct artillery fire, stuff like that. It seemed like nice quiet work at the time and I was really good at the aerial photography. I've got these great eyes, remember? And to fly! You're in this old Farnham trainer, sounds like a tractor. It coughs, wheezes, chugs its way up to one thousand feet. You're in a kite with a motor that can barely get off the ground. But even so, you're in the air... You're not on the ground. You're above everything.

The piano player plays some mess-hall music.

It was a different world up there. A different war and a different breed of men fighting that war... Flyers! During training we heard all the stories. If you went down behind enemy lines and were killed, they'd come over, the Germans that is, under a flag of truce and drop a photograph of your grave. Nice. If you were taken prisoner, it was the champagne razzle in the mess. Talking and drinking all night. It was a different war they were fighting up there. And from where I stood, it looked pretty darn good.

* * *

SECTION FOUR — GO, CAT, GO!

Of the twelve characters you will meet in these last, complex scenes, less than half of them are close to your age. That means you will have to do some serious observing of the older generation. Adults move differently, react differently and speak differently than teenagers - that's what makes them so weird. A good actor can re-create these differences on stage.

Secondly, some of these scenes are set in the past. Re-creating a time period in theatre is primarily the job of the set designer and costumer. Since *you are both*, discuss with your partner small ways in which you can help the audience see into the past - often one simple **hand prop**, or well chosen piece of **intro music** - can firmly set the scene for the audience, and help you communicate all the ideas in the drama.

Lastly, these scenes are all-dressed, combination take-outs - there are enough dramatic layers to challenge you considerably. There are **technical aspects** in **sound** and **lighting, set** and **costume**; there are **staging elements** of **pacing, comic timing** and **movement**; there are **character skills** of the **body (gestures, reactions, physicalization)** and of the **voice (inflection, tone, pause).** But, don't let the terms throw you; the only theory question you and your partner must answer before performance is simple. As you read and enjoy the moments of each scene, ask yourself how am I going to get *that* across to the audience? The answer to that question is always found in one of the toppings above.

Scene 34

"Sibyl and Sylvia"

by Colleen Curran

2 females

    Colleen Curran is Montreal novelist and playwright. She likes to write comedy. Sibyl and Sylvia, sisters who are "total opposites", and have recently come into a wealthy inheritance, provide the **comic scenario** for this selection. By the way, this is Colleen's first play, written when she was in high school.

    One key to the successful staging of this scene, which is actually a self-contained short play, is creating a Sylvia who is "a flamboyant woman of the world", completely at home in her "old, feudal castle" with her aristocratic friends. Characters such as this one fill a room (even a large room in a castle) when they enter. This, and a good, aristocratic voice, all slightly exaggerated for **comic effect**, will give you an amusing Sylvia. It is important to imagine her sister Sibyl as more than "non-flamboyant" or "uninteresting" by comparison. Good writers like Colleen Curran leave lots of clues in the **dialogue** about their characters — we know Sibyl is a writer, is sensitive to "vibrations", and shows little concern for Sylvia's new wealth. Both are sisters, though, are capable of murdering each other, and their comic attempts at this action which create most of the comedy.

    There are several hand props which are essential to the scene: the gun, the tea cups, the books, the "poison" — make sure you have at least one **dress rehearsal** using these items. A window is the only other necessary set piece and, after reading the final stage direction, I can only wish you luck.

Sibyl and Sylvia

Somewhere in the south of England. The setting is the sparsely but finely furnished living room of an old feudal castle. There is a window upstage and a couch placed centre stage. There's a table with a typewriter and mystery thriller books and attempts at writing scattered about. Partially-read newspapers are on the floor and on the couch.

As the play begins, SIBYL is eating toast and reading a newspaper with grisly headlines with great interest. There is a knock at the door and SIBYL jumps up nervously to answer it. Before she can do so, her sister SYLVIA, a flamboyant woman of the world, enters. They are total opposites of each other.

SYLVIA   I let myself in. I've just come to tell you that you must leave the castle.

SIBYL   You always were subtle, Sylvia.

SYLVIA   Yes... As you know dearheart, Daddy left me this little spot, hidden in the countryside, as part of his will.

SIBYL   I know he did.

SYLVIA   And since he did, you must vacate the premises immediately. It was fine for you to lock yourself up here while Daddy was alive but you can't anymore. You leave today.

SIBYL   But I can't. You know I need this castle.

SYLVIA   Please Sibyl, begging is very unbecoming on you.

SIBYL   But it isn't fair.

SYLVIA   Oh no, now it is fair! It was unfair when Daddy was alive. But now Daddy's Precious has finally received her fair share: Nothing!

SIBYL   He did leave me his Love & Good Fortune.

SYLVIA   And he left me two million pounds and all his properties including this tacky little estate.

SIBYL   If it's so tacky, why are you so determined to make me leave?

SYLVIA   Because I can rent it out.

SIBYL   You've already got two million pounds. What could a little rent do for you?

SYLVIA   Plenty. I've rented this place to the Baron von Austerlitz.

SIBYL   That prig!

SYLVIA   He's not a pig. And besides he can pay for his residency here. What did you do with all the furniture, sell it?

SIBYL   Look, I only need the castle for one more month. Then I'll be sure to finish my book.

SYLVIA   Oh, that study you've been doing for the past three years on the History of the English Countryside?

SYLVIA has wandered over to the table with SIBYL's writing.

You can finish it off in some little garret room in London. Anyway the Baron and his entourage are arriving in two days. That should give you time to move out your things.

SIBYL	But I need this place.
SYLVIA	You said that before.
SIBYL	But I do. It gives me inspiration. Where will I go? You know I have no money.
SYLVIA	Don't worry. I'm perfectly aware of that fact.
SIBYL	But I need this house — just for a month.
SYLVIA	No. No. *NO!*
SIBYL	But the vibrations this castle gives off...
SYLVIA	It's only a draft.
SIBYL	(*lying*) But it does give off vibrations... You know the original owner ... a Lord Phillip jumped out that very window when he saw that the castle was being besieged by ... the Normans or the Huns or someone.
SYLVIA	Are you treating me to the Points of Interest chapter of your book, Sibyl?
SIBYL	No. I just thought that you might be interested.
SYLVIA	Why should I be interested in that?
SIBYL	I just thought that you might be interested. He jumped right out that window ... and died of course.
SYLVIA	Oh, of course. The story wouldn't be complete unless he died. But Sibyl, we're on the ground floor.
SIBYL	Yes.
SYLVIA	He jumped from the first storey and killed himself?

SIBYL	You see the moat is very deep.
SYLVIA	What moat?
SIBYL	There is one, you know. Would you like some coffee?
SYLVIA	How civil of you, Sibyl. Yes, I'd love some.
SIBYL	You are quite certain that I have to leave the castle?
SYLVIA	Yes. If you had enough money to purchase it. I might reconsider but ...
SIBYL	But circumstances being what they are, you simply have to let the Baron have the Castle ...
SYLVIA	Yes.
SIBYL	Oh alright then. I'll get the coffee.
SYLVIA	And I won't even charge you for the use of my cooker.
SIBYL	There is a moat there, you know ... Oh yes the coffee.
	SIBYL exits.
SYLVIA	What moat?
	SYLVIA saunters over to the window and puts her head out, holding the window sill. Meanwhile SIBYL is creeping up behind her and just as she is about to push her, SYLVIA turns. SIBYL catches herself, takes a deep breath and says
SIBYL	We only have cream, will that be alright?
SYLVIA	(*shocked*) Yes!

SIBYL makes a move to leave the room again.

SYLVIA "We"? What did you mean by that "We only have cream"?

SIBYL Just that we have only cream. I know you always hated cream in or on anything when you were at home ...

SYLVIA You know that's not what I meant. You said "We" — what did you mean by that?

SIBYL Oh, did I say "We"? My, I didn't even realize that I had. It must be the vibrations. The ghost of Sir Phillip. I won't say "We" anymore if it bothers you.

SYLVIA I don't understand you.

SIBYL And why is that, dearest?

SYLVIA One minute you're practically in tears because I won't let you stay here and the next you're flitting around like a sixteen-year old. You act as if you're glad you're leaving ...

SIBYL But I won't be leaving.

SYLVIA You won't be leaving...

SIBYL My lighter ... I won't be leaving my lighter. I must show it to you.

SIBYL begins rummaging among the papers.

It's quite clever really. I went to the Edgar Awards. It was presented to me by Cecil Hardstock because he said I had a brilliantly clever and criminal mind. That's why I'm writing my new book here, it's a thriller — a murder mystery...

SYLVIA   Oh my, don't tell me that little Sibyl fosters notions of being the new Agatha Christie. At least then you could support yourself. Because Daddy won't anymore!

SIBYL   Oh, I have other plans for taking care of that, Sylvia. Where is it? Oh, now I know where it is ... I'll be right back, duckie.

SIBYL exits.

SYLVIA   "Duckie"? Sibyl, what are you doing? Come back here!

SIBYL comes back, carrying a gun pointed at SYLVIA.

SYLVIA   (*sits very stiff*) Ahh, ahh ... is that what he gave you.

SIBYL   Yes ... What did Mr. Drew-Bear say after I ran out in tears?

SYLVIA   Drew-Bear? Oh yes, the lawyer ... He just said a lot of rot about "in the event of death all possessions pass on to the nearest relative".

SYLVIA grabs gun.

Let me see that gun. I mean, lighter. I should so like to try it. I'd swear it was a gun. You're right. It really is quite clever.

SIBYL   Yes it is, isn't it? Point it this way and you'll see the flame.

SIBYL has aimed it at SYLVIA's head, forcing her hand.

SYLVIA   Why don't point it like ... this?

SYLVIA points it at SIBYL.

SIBYL   Yes. Don't point it at me!

SYLVIA But don't you want to see the flame, Sibyl?

SIBYL   I've seen it before...

SYLVIA But I want to see how it works ... Let me light your cigarette for you.

SIBYL   No. No! I... I... I don't smoke anymore. I quit. Bad for the lungs.

SYLVIA Oh, do you have a candle? I should so like to light something with it.

SIBYL   No candles, anywhere... Oh, here, let me have the gun, I mean lighter... I'll get the coffee.

SYLVIA You get the coffee. I'd like to look at it some more.

SIBYL   Alright.

SIBYL warily begins to make her way off stage, watching the gloating SYLVIA.

Here. I looked at it long enough.

SYLVIA tosses the gun past SIBYL, off stage. There is a loud gunshot.

Oh my. You brought the wrong gun. That one was real . I could have killed you. I'm so sorry.

SIBYL   Oh, that's all right. How I made such a mistake...

SYLVIA ...you'll never know ... get the coffee. NOW.

SIBYL exits. As soon as she's gone, SYLVIA takes a small packet out of her purse. She

>   *hides it in her skirt. Enter SIBYL with coffee*
>   *on a nice tray with good tea cups, etc.*

SIBYL   Here we are. This cup is nicer than that one so you may have it. It's kind of whitish on top because of the refined sugar I use. Mine isn't whitish because I don't like sugar ...

SYLVIA   Oh. How nice of you. Oh! I've got something in my eye. Look!

SIBYL   I can't see anything.

SYLVIA   Look closely,

>   *SYLVIA slips something from small packet*
>   *into SIBYL's coffee.*

Oh well, it's gone now. Let's drink to my fortune and your bad. (*laughs*)

SIBYL   To my Love & Good Fortune, and that which is to come! Ahh, my books of course.

SYLVIA   What a strange taste. Very chalky ...

SIBYL   That must be because of the sugar.

SYLVIA   Sibyl your sugar has gone rancid. Drink your coffee.

SIBYL   Oh I will. (*drinks some*) Oh. I don't remember putting sugar in my coffee.

SYLVIA   Doesn't yours taste good?

SIBYL   No, it's terribly bitter.

SYLVIA   How strange. Perhaps your cream is rancid, too.

SIBYL   Maybe. Maybe I'd better go check it. I'd hate to get sick.

SYLVIA Oh, you won't get sick. Stay here. I have something to tell you. You know that all Daddy left you was his Love & Good Fortune?

SIBYL (*her eyes beginning to wander as if she's about to pass out*) Yes ...

SYLVIA Well after you ran out of the lawyer's office, Mr. Drew-Bear read the rest of the will. Daddy, you see, was unfair to me even in the end. Love & Good Fortune is a chain of hotels and restaurants in America! You know how coy Americans can be in naming things. Anyway Love & Good Fortune according to Daddy's obituary in *Fortune Magazine* are reputedly worth well over three hundred and sixty million pounds. Funny, eh? We always thought that Daddy had either spent the money or gambled it away.

SYLVIA is now starting to get dizzy, too.

SIBYL Oh how wonderful! I'll publish my own books! No more rejection slips! All that and your two million pounds, too!

SYLVIA What are you talking about?

SIBYL I poisoned your drink.

SYLVIA No, I poisoned yours! You don't actually expect me to believe that you would do that too, do you?

SIBYL I did poison your drink, you know. Quite merciful stuff, too. It makes you dizzy then reacts all of a sudden. Any last words?

SYLVIA (*realizing that she is dizzy*) Don't pull that on me ... I'm not your Sir Phillip. My nerves aren't that bad. So stop counting on me jumping out that window into your two foot moat. I've known since I got here that you'd try something. But I'm ahead of you ... I planted poison in this mud that you're trying to pass off as coffee. Did you really think I wasn't on to that cute "lighter" trick? How crude! If you had such a brilliantly clever mind I'm sure that you would have tried something a little more artistic. You'll be leaving me all your Love & Good Fortune very shortly... The poison leaves no trace. "Your Honour, I told the Dear One that she'd inherited three hundred and sixty million pounds and she fainted dead away. I shall try to run those American hotels and restaurants as she would have..."

I shall play the role of the grieving sister... Why are you smiling? I poisoned your coffee ...criminal mind! Ha Ha...

SYLVIA smiles then suddenly gags.

(*realizes*) You really could have been more original, Sibyl ...

SYLVIA falls and her last words are:

It was my idea first!

SYLVIA is dead. SIBYL is dizzy.

SIBYL   To think Love & Good Fortune was really hotels! Oh, I must think up a good excuse for the police ... I know! "She didn't know what to do with all those extra pounds ... she begged me to take them and when I refused she said, 'All right! I'll make you take them!' and she flung herself out the window into the moat!"

SIBYL has dragged SYLVIA's body over to the window.

"She died, of course, leaving me her millions and millions".

SIBYL is about to toss SYLVIA out the window.

(*gags suddenly*) Oh! Oh my! I wonder if the cream was rancid after all!

SIBYL breathes her last and falls out the window and into the moat taking her sister with her.

* * *

Scene 35

"Donne In"

by Yvette Nolan

2 males

    Yvette Nolan writes plays, performs, directs and teaches. Her mother is Algonquin and Yvette's interest in Native drama led her into the post of first-ever writer-in-residence for the education of Native teachers at Brandon University, Manitoba.

    "Donne In" is a **comedy** about a suicide attempt. You can see Yvette Nolan likes a challenge. A man named Donne is talked down from the railing of a bridge by a friendly cabbie named Max, who sees him from his car. In the process, they cover such topics as poetry, Buddhism and the taste of good scotch. What more could you ask?

DONNE IN
_____

>*Night. A man stands on the railing of a bridge looking down at the water. He leans out over the water, hanging on with one hand.*
>
>*Sound of a car door. MAX enters behind DONNE.*

MAX   Huyah!

DONNE   Aaauch! (*he grabs the upright and clings*) Christ!

MAX   Couldn't do it, eh? That was your big chance.

DONNE   What the hell are you talking about?

MAX   Could even've told yourself it was an accident on the way down. In case you're a Catholic.

DONNE   I'm not — I'm not — I wasn't going to... (*pause*) I was chased up here by a dog.

MAX   A dog.

DONNE   Yes, a dog.

MAX   What kind of a dog?

DONNE   Why?

MAX   I mean, was it a little white dog? A boxer? A pit bull? Did it bite you? Was it drooling and foaming?

DONNE   Black. It was black. With teeth.

MAX   With teeth, eh?

MAX looks around.

MAX Well, I don't see any dog around here, white, black or otherwise. Why don't you come down?

DONNE Look, why don't you— Thank you very much for your concern, but I am fine, so if you could please just leave me alone.

MAX I can't do that.

DONNE Oh. Why? Why not?

MAX I can't just leave you here, thinking about — you know.

DONNE I told you, it was a dog.

MAX Right. Well, I can't leave you here, thinking about dogs.

DONNE Why not? What are you supposed to be? An angel?

MAX Cabbie.

DONNE Pardon?

MAX I'm a cabdriver. A cabbie. Just a cabbie on the graveyard shift looking for a fare, deader'n shit out here, I see this guy standing on the railing of a bridge, I figure, there's a guy that needs a lift.

DONNE Well, I don't.

MAX Look like you do.

DONNE Well, I don't. Okay? So could you just go away, Mr.-Graveyard-Shift-Just-Looking-For-a-Fare?

MAX Max.

DONNE	Max?
MAX	Max. My name.
DONNE	Oh.
MAX	Yours?
DONNE	Donne.
MAX	Done? No wonder you're trying to check out.
DONNE	Donne. Like the poet.
MAX	"Do not go gently into that good night..."
DONNE	That's Dylan Thomas.
MAX	Oh. "Death be not proud..."
DONNE	That's the one. (*pause*) Are you sure you're a cabbie?
MAX	You mean, because I know some poetry? What, you think I woke up as a fourteen year old one fresh morning a coupla hundred years ago and thought, Doctor? Lawyer? Naw, I'm gonna be a cabdriver when I grow up.
DONNE	No, I didn't mean, Well, I didn't think— well, maybe I did.
MAX	But you know, shit happens. Shit just happens. Or as my Buddhist friend says, shit happens for a reason.
DONNE	Great. Just great. Zen and the art of cab-driving.
MAX	Oh c'm'on Donne. Get it? Come on Donne. Come on down. Come on down, Donne. I bet you got teased a lot as a kid. Dun-da-duh-dun. (*Oh oh music theme*) Dun-de-de-dun-de-

	de-dun dun (*"Bonanza" theme*). (*pretends to knock*) Are you Donne in there?
DONNE	Okay, that's it. (*he starts to step off the railing*)
MAX	Wait! Please! Please, I'm not going about this the right way. I do that, always make a joke, try and lighten up the situation. It's not always appreciated.
DONNE	Please. Just go away.
MAX	I can't do that.
DONNE	Why?
MAX	I just can't.
	Pause.
MAX	Look, Donne. I'm not going to give you any grand speeches about sunrises and the laughter of a child, the taste of good scotch or your mama's scalloped potatoes, about that first sip of coffee in the morning, about the unconditional love of a dog—
	DONNE glares at him.
MAX	Okay. okay, bad example. Anyway, I'm not doing that speech because I know you don't give a rat's ass about any of those things right now. In fact, there's not all that much to recommend this life. It's hard, and it's lonely, and it's ... it's...
	MAX stops, sighs. Pause.
DONNE	Max?
MAX	Yuh.
DONNE	It's ...?

MAX   What?

DONNE   You were giving me a speech about not giving me a speech about flowers and sunsets and all that crap—

MAX   Flowers and sunsets? I never said anything about flowers and sunsets.

DONNE   Yeah, okay, whatever, not flowers and sunsets but, you know, clichés, and then you said it's hard and lonely and you ... stopped.

MAX   Yeah, well, got wore out thinking about it.

DONNE   You're not very good at this, Max.

MAX   So, what do you care? You're gonna go for the big swim anyway, leave me standing here looking like the biggest jerk in the universe.

DONNE   I don't care, really, it's just if you're going to try and reach out to someone who is contemplating the big swim, as you so colourfully put it, you might want to work on your technique a little.

MAX   So what are you gonna do, haunt me?

DONNE   Don't.

MAX   Don't what?

DONNE   Don't get cynical and bitter on me, You're not like that.

MAX   No, I'm not. How do you know?

DONNE   Because you stopped. Because you stopped to try and talk a guy down off a bridge. Because you're a *cabbie* who stopped.

MAX   Now look who's getting bitter and cynical.

DONNE   I'm the guy who's jumping, I'm allowed. Supposed to, in fact.

MAX   But you're not now, are you.

DONNE looks down at the water.

MAX   'Cause you see, the thing is, Donne, it's not as bad now as it was ten minutes ago, is it? And in ten more minutes, it'll probably be not as bad as it seems now. It's not as dramatic as sunrise, just ... passes ... a little bit.

Pause. DONNE shakes his head.

MAX   C'mon, you're not going to go through with it because you said you would and you're a stand-up kind of guy who always follows through. No one knows, right? So, no one will ever know, I won't tell anyone.

DONNE   Oh yeah, you'll dine out on this for a month, It'll be the topper story down at the donut shop, won't it? So I'm driving along, s'deader than shit, and I see this guy standing on the bridge, this *suit*, that's what you'll call me, right MAX? This *suit*, and he says he's been chased up there by a dog — and all your little friends will go har-de-har-de-har.

MAX   I won't tell anyone.

DONNE   Of course you will, and you'll all relish the fact that there's really nothing wrong with my life, that I have it all, the car, the job, okay so I can't get past the second date, and I haven't touched another human being in six months, but so what? I'm not hungry, I've got my health, and you'll all shake your heads and go, 'Aw, poor little yuppie feels empty...'

MAX   I won't tell anyone.

DONNE	Sure you will. I would.
MAX	You're not me.
DONNE	No.
MAX	Come down and we'll go for a cup a coffee. Pass the next half hour or so. Talk poetry. We're both poetry guys. You know Hopkins?
DONNE	"Not, I'll not, carrion comfort, Despair—
MAX	"Not feast on thee—". Good poet.
DONNE	Great poet.
MAX	Also kinda down. Jesuit.
DONNE	You a Catholic?
MAX	Me? God no! Grew out of it.
	DONNE laughs.
MAX	Come on down, Donne.
DONNE	Okay.
	He does not move.
MAX	Shoo! Git' G'wan! Okay, coast's clear. No dog.
	DONNE looks at him. MAX offers him a hand. DONNE jumps down.
MAX	My cab's over here.
DONNE	Streets really are dead.
	A church bell chimes five o'clock.

MAX	Five o'clock. Sun'll be up in half an hour. C'mon, we wanna beat the breakfast rush.
DONNE	Okay.
MAX	And my friends don't go har-de-har-de-har.
DONNE	I didn't mean anything.
MAX	That would be evil.
DONNE	I just meant—

They exit.

* * *

Scene 36

"I Am Marguerite"

by Shirley Barrie

2 females

The author writes...

"In 1542, 19-year-old Marguerite de Roberval contrived to join her brother Jean Francois "Sieur" de Roberval, on the great expedition to found the first French colony in the New World. But, when Jean Francois discovered that she had fallen in love with an unsuitable young nobleman on board ship, he abandoned Marguerite on a deserted island in the Strait of Belle Isle for daring to choose love over duty."

This little-known but true story is the subject of Shirley Barrie's play. In the following scene, Marguerite has been abandoned at Belle Isle and her distress has caused her to recall an incident two and one half years ago. During this *flashback*, her "practical and devoted Nurse", Damienne, attempts to persuade her to attend a ball in the court of the Queen of Navarre.

Damienne's entrance cues the **flashback** to begin. Marguerite's lines before the entrance offer a **transition** from present to past, and Shirley Barrie uses the dress (an essential **prop**) to spark Marguerite's memory. When Damienne exits, Marguerite's last line refers to both her past and present circumstances. It is ironic.

The scene reminds me, at least, of Juliet waiting anxiously for her Nurse to return with words from Romeo only Marguerite's anxiety is created out of frustration and anger, not romantic expectation.

I Am Marguerite

MARGUERITE has just shot at the phantom of her brother, and is terrified that the sailors who have anchored off shore have heard the noise. Seeing the dinghy being lowered makes MARGUERITE flip into the past to her time at court before she left for The New World.

MARGUERITE   What if they heard? If they heard, they'll know... And I can't ... I can't...

She tears off the dress which the Queen had persuaded her to put on.

They're going to lower a dinghy! *(a horrified pause)* The sailors were checking the ropes when Damienne and I were brought on deck... Eugene was between two sailors. For a moment I dared to hope that Jean-Francois was going to let us ... But there was no priest.

DAMIENNE enters.

DAMIENNE   It's time you were getting dressed. *(she picks up the dress)*

MARGUERITE   *(turning away)* No!

DAMIENNE   If you don't put this on now, I won't have time to curl your hair. *(pause)* I hear they have some new musicians for the dancing.

MARGUERITE   I won't go.

DAMIENNE   The Queen of Navarre is expecting you. You can't disappoint... *(holding out the dress)*

MARGUERITE   *(slipping into the past)* I've worn that old rag a hundred times.

DAMIENNE	I'm almost finished the new collar.
MARGUERITE	I don't want a new collar. I want a new gown!
DAMIENNE	I'm sorry, mademoiselle but... (your brother...)
MARGUERITE	We're not poor, Damienne. Why won't he give me the money for a decent dress?
DAMIENNE	*(trying to put the dress over MARGUERITE's head)* You always enjoy the dancing.
MARGUERITE	*(grabbing at the dress and throwing it down)* I hate it.
DAMIENNE	It will be all dusty.
MARGUERITE	The men are choosing me last for the dances. I'm 19 years old and already I'm sitting in the line with the old women. My life is over!!
DAMIENNE	How can you say such a thing?
MARGUERITE	I've been here at court a whole year, and there hasn't been one offer of marriage for me. Not one.
DAMIENNE	Oh now you mustn't be thinking that, Marguerite. *(breaking off, she gives a final brush to the dress)* No harm done. Put it on, now.
MARGUERITE	Tell me, Damienne.
DAMIENNE	It's really not my place...
MARGUERITE	*(grabbing her arm brutally)* Tell me!!
DAMIENNE	I've ... I've heard...
MARGUERITE	What!

DAMIENNE   Ow! They say...

MARGUERITE Who says?

DAMIENNE   You know as there's always talk among the servants.

MARGUERITE Wonderful! My life is subject matter for kitchen gossip.

> *She slips the dress over MARGUERITE's head.*

DAMIENNE   I spoke out of turn, Mademoiselle.

MARGUERITE Tell me what they're saying about me in the kitchens.

DAMIENNE   There's probably no truth to...

MARGUERITE Don't presume to judge the truth for me.

DAMIENNE   They say that there's been offers.

MARGUERITE Of marriage?

DAMIENNE   Very good ones in the normal course of things. But your brother's turned them all down. So you see it's nothing to do with you.

MARGUERITE Why has he turned them down?

DAMIENNE   I wouldn't presume to judge....

MARGUERITE Don't be impertinent or I'll send you back to Perigord.

DAMIENNE   They say ... your brother...

MARGUERITE Yes.

DAMIENNE   ... needs a lot more money to fit up the ships he's taking to the new world. He's in big debt...

MARGUERITE   Jean-Francois won't let me marry because he doesn't want to pay the dowry!

DAMIENNE   I'm only a servant... I don't know....

MARGUERITE   *(running over DAMIENNE's last line)* And you knew! And you didn't tell me!

DAMIENNE   I thought as long as you were happy...

MARGUERITE   He's going to go adventuring off to The New World for years, and leave me here — an old maid with one dress!! *(a break)* I began this whole venture because I didn't like my wardrobe?! *(DAMIENNE smiles)* How dare you suggest such a...

DAMIENNE   I suggested nothing.

MARGUERITE   I won't listen to you.

DAMIENNE   Fine. *(she starts to leave)*

MARGUERITE   Don't leave me!

DAMIENNE stops. Throws up her hands in exasperation. MARGUERITE rushes to the trunk and gets out a brush.

Brush my hair? Like you used to...

MARGUERITE sits down and holds up the brush. DAMIENNE takes it and begins to brush.

MARGUERITE   Ouch!

DAMIENNE   I never could keep the tangles out. I think your brother sent you off to that convent so young because I couldn't keep you looking like a de Roberval.

MARGUERITE   He had no idea how stupid those nuns were.

DAMIENNE	God forgive you, Marguerite.
MARGUERITE	They only had two punishments: Hail Mary's forever or helping the old gardener.
DAMIENNE	Sit still now. I can't...
MARGUERITE	"Oh, please, Mother Agnes," I'd cry, "don't send me to the garden. I'll get my dress all dirty and it's so hard to get the dirt out from under my nails."
DAMIENNE	Is that why you've let the vegetable patch go to seed? After we worked so hard....
MARGUERITE	"Such vanity, child," Sister would say, "You will go to the garden today and tomorrow." *(she laughs)*
DAMIENNE	Well you always did have a knack for getting what you wanted.
MARGUERITE	You think I wanted this?!
DAMIENNE	No.
MARGUERITE	I wanted.... I wanted.....
	DAMIENNE looks at her with sorrowful affection and leaves.
MARGUERITE	*(struggling to understand)* I wanted..... *(hearing the music of the court)* I wanted to dance.

* * *

Scene 37

from "Nurse Jane Goes to Hawaii"

by Allan Stratton

1 female / 1 male

PASSION AND DESIRE

  In the precious, difficult, even undervalued, world of comedy-writing, **farce** is king. A **farce** is a comedy filled with unlikely characters stuck in impossible fixes with absolutely no time to get out before they get caught, multiplied four or five times. You've no doubt seen movies or TV shows where the only thing stopping you from jumping into the screen and warning the silly fool of impending social disaster is the delicious treat of *watching* them get caught and totally embarrassed, and thanking God you weren't involved! That is **farce**. The term comes from the French theatre and means "stuffed" — comedy so stuffed with improbabilities that we just have to laugh.

  This early play by Allan Stratton is a masterful **farce**, proven by the mere fact that this play has had over 300 productions, from Alaska to New York. His other plays include the triple award winner, "Rexy!" (Dora Mavor Moore Award, Chalmers Award, Canadian Authors' Association Award), "Papers" (Chalmers Award; Dora Mavor Moore Award nomination; and the Governor General's Literary Award), and "Bag Babies" (Toronto Book Award nomination). He has been writing successfully for over twenty years.

  This is the opening scene. Believing that his wife, Doris, is away for the weekend, Edgar enters his well-appointed home with Vivien, a flirtatious, yet virginal, writer of Harlequin Romances. *He* hopes to have to have an affair; *she* hopes finally to lose her virginity. Of course, Edgar's wife, Doris, an advice columnist, is not any further away than the next room. These facts, together with seeing the boring, practical Edgar against the totally flaky Vivien, makes any audience laugh. Oh, did I mention the hula-dancing? Aloha.

Nurse Jane Goes to Hawaii

        DORIS exits into the bathroom humming, closing the door behind her. No sooner is the bathroom door closed than EDGAR CHISHOLM and VIVIEN BLISS enter through the front door. EDGAR, DORIS' husband, is a rumpled man in grey flannels. Shy and awkward, he thinks he is in love with VIVIEN, mid-thirties, a delightfully flighty writer of Harlequin romance novels. She carries a portable tape recorder over her shoulder.

VIVIEN   (*looking around the living room*) Why, Edgar, it's so ritzy. It's like I always dreamed it would be! I mean it's Bungalow City! Oh, but I feel wicked.

EDGAR   May I take your coat?

VIVIEN   Not yet. Just let me breathe in the *je ne sais quoi*. Oh my, an Eskimo carving. Did you make it?

EDGAR   Just into ceramics I'm afraid.

VIVIEN   How cruel of me not to notice them first. I spy with my little eye something beginning with 'ashtray.' (*picking up ceramic*) I remember when this came out of the kiln. Oh, but I admire your textures. I like the way they seem to say, 'Hello, little cigarette, I'm going to hold you in ways you've never dreamed!'

EDGAR   Yes. And there's the typewriter. With Doris in Windsor it's yours for the weekend.

VIVIEN (*indicating tape recorder*] Thanks, but I've got Constant Companion. He's taped all my novels and I mustn't be unfaithful. Bad luck. Oh — there's one of your abstracts! (*goes to woe-begone piece of clay*)

EDGAR Very rough.

VIVIEN YES! Why, it looks like Hawaii!

EDGAR Pardon?

VIVIEN Little volcanoes all over. I can almost see the palm trees.

EDGAR Doris thinks it should go in the garbage.

VIVIEN She doesn't even like this one?

EDGAR When company comes she packs them all up in a box in the basement. Says she doesn't want to see me embarrassed

VIVIEN The cad-ess. Why must we artists suffer at such unfeeling hands? Let me comfort.

She embraces him.

EDGAR Vivien.

VIVIEN (*releasing*) Oh, Edgar, isn't it strange and wonderful and beautiful, the two of us? You, geography teacher by day, artist by night; me, a novelist of passion and romance seeking intrigue; each guided by some Unseen Hand to an extension course in ceramics at the Ontario College of Art! Oh, Edgar - (*they are about to kiss*) I want a drink.

EDGAR Whiskey Sour?

VIVIEN You're a psychic!

EDGAR And would you care for a seat?

VIVIEN   Thank you but no. I'm still exploring this playground of adventure.

EDGAR   Good.

                They blow each other kisses and he exits into the kitchen.

VIVIEN   (*looks around the room, then says to a ceramic*) Hello Hawaii. EUREKA! TELEPHONE! BETTY! WHERE'S THE — HAWAII (*she touchtones furiously*) Ceramics live, they breath. They — they — oh thank you Edgar — (*into phone*) Harlequin? This is Vivien Bliss... Yes I know my novel was due yesterday. DON'T YELL AT ME, I'M IN PROCESS! Tell Betty I'm luxuriating with my paramour at 16 The Bridle Path. Tell her it's paradise and I'm calling it "Nurse Jane Goes To Hawaii". I can see it now lagoons, Ferraris and tsetse flies. 'Bye! (*hangs up, to tape recorder*) "Nurse Jane Goes To Hawaii". Chapter One. Nurse Jane sighed. Paragraph. She had just arrived in Honolulu from Pleasantville Hospital for an International Symposium on Malaria. And she had met the continental Dr. Edgar Sterling from Britain. He had a strikingly cleft, jutting chin, piercing blue eyes that danced and a silver tie clip on which was emblazoned his family crest. 'Oh, to call him Ed instead of Dr. Sterling,' she mused, as they strolled along the shore, listening to the crashing waves while porpoises whistled playfully beyond the coral reef. Paragraph. An aged denizen approached. 'Aloha. You might please to join our luau,' he inquired. Dr. Sterling replied in the affirmative and guided Nurse Jane into the nearby bamboo hut with professional ease. Chapter Two.

> *EDGAR re-enters from the kitchen with a tray on which are two Whiskey Sours and a rye bottle.*

Suddenly Nurse Jane found herself plied with exotic libations.

EDGAR   Here we are.

VIVIEN   (*to tape*) ...'said Dr. Sterling.'

EDGAR   (*offering drink*) Pardon?

VIVIEN   (taking drink, to tape) 'Thank you,' she replied huskily.

EDGAR   Vivien?

VIVIEN   (*to tape*) What were his intentions, she pondered with fluttering heart.

EDGAR   Vivien??? (*touches her*)

VIVIEN   (*to tape*) Dr. Sterling advanced.

EDGAR   Are you all right?

VIVIEN   (*to tape*) 'I've never been better,' she breathed. An inner voice beckoned. It said—

EDGAR   Are you sure?

VIVIEN   (*waving him off, to tape*) It said... (*turning tape off*) Never mind, it's gone.

EDGAR   Gone?

VIVIEN   (*realizing he doesn't understand*) Sorry. My novel.

EDGAR   I interrupted?

VIVIEN   It's not your fault. It's ... what can I say?

They clink glasses. He sips. Unaccustomed to drinking, she finishes hers in one slow, steady swallow.

EDGAR (*beat*) Can I get you anything else?

VIVIEN (*trying to recover the thread of her novel*) I'm not sure.

EDGAR Perhaps some music?

VIVIEN Oh! Love songs!

EDGAR Perry Como, Herb Alpert, Tony Bennett...

VIVIEN No, you!

EDGAR Me?

VIVIEN Sing to me, Edgar! Put me in the mood. We'll dance while you sing.

EDGAR Vivien ... have we had a little too much?

VIVIEN No such thing as too much.

EDGAR But...

VIVIEN Pretty please? For, me? Your inspiration? You're so cute where you say that. Come on.

VIVIEN sings the first line of a popular romantic upbeat Hawaiian song. She looks expectantly at EDGAR who awkwardly repeats it. As she exuberantly continues the song, she motions him to sing along, which he attempts to do, repeating the last word or phrase of each line with great embarrassment in an unintentional parody of an Hawaiian lounge act. As the song builds, VIVIEN adds hula-hula dance movements which EDGAR, mortified, attempts to copy. At the finale, she hits a high note and collapses on the couch.

VIVIEN   Gosh, I'm possessed. Thank you.

EDGAR   Vivien ...

VIVIEN   Ah hah? (*winks*)

EDGAR   I ... look, I'm sorry.

VIVIEN   What about?

EDGAR   This wasn't such a good idea.

VIVIEN   But you sing so well.

EDGAR   Not that. It's just that I've never... I mean I don't know what I should be doing. I mean, Doris was the first girl I ever dated and what am I saying? I was married once before, for heaven's sake. To my first wife, Betty. But that was a whirlwind affair, a matter of weeks actually, because of my ... habit. I was obsessed with Atmospheric Optics — reams of charts and statistics which Betty would throw in the air—

VIVIEN   Say no more. My editor's a Betty too, and she's a terror.

EDGAR   Forget your editor. Forget Betty. What I'm trying to say is — I feel like a fool.

VIVIEN   Why?

EDGAR   Never mind. I'll drive you home.

VIVIEN   But you said we'd have the weekend. You promised and I've told Harlequin I'm here and — oh Edgar, this weekend means so much to me!

EDGAR   You don't have to pretend.

VIVIEN   But I want to pretend. And with you. All weekend. Passion, desire, romance... (*pause*) It's something I've done, isn't it? I've done something?

EDGAR   No, no, you've been delightful. It's me.

VIVIEN   You don't have to lie. I always do something. Always. I meet someone really interesting, a kindred spirit, someone I love who I think loves me — and I meet them everywhere at weaving class, pottery class, life-drawing class — my life is class after class after class. And it always ends up the same. I get in the door having a wonderful time, thinking we're getting along famously, and all of a sudden I'm back in the car being driven home and he won't even look at me. And I let myself in and go up to my bedsitter, praying Miss Clement won't ask how the date went — and she keeps her hearing aid low so you practically have to *scream* "I failed again" to all the neighbours — and I go into my room and rummage about in my hope chest, through quilts, linen, stitch-work — or maybe just stare at the one corsage I ever got to press in my Bible. And I have a good cry. Because I don't know what I've done — they never say. And it must be me because it's always the same. Then I pull out a Kleenex and turn on the tape and talk about Nurse Jane and her exciting adventures. And it's not fair! I'm a virgin, damnit, and it's not fair! Of course so is Nurse Jane — but at least she gets more than a parting embrace. (*she turns away*)

EDGAR   (*quietly*) Vivien ... I'm sorry.

VIVIEN   Don't tell me you're sorry. I'm tired of people saying they're sorry. Do you have a subway token?

EDGAR   No, Vivien, no.

VIVIEN	That's OK. I can hitch-hike. (*goes to the front door*)
EDGAR	No, Vivien, please — stay with me?
VIVIEN	Very good of you, but I don't need mercy. And besides, the linen needs ironing.
EDGAR	Vivien, I... Look at me? Vivien? (*she does*) Stay with me? Please?
VIVIEN	(*throws herself in his arms*) Oh, Edgar!
EDGAR	I though you thought I was a boring old fool.
VIVIEN	Edgar, you're the most marvellous man I ever met.
EDGAR	And make sure you catch Miss Clement in the hall Sunday night.
VIVIEN	'I did it, Miss Clement. I did it!'
EDGAR	(*as Miss Clement*) 'Eh?'
VIVIEN	I'm a fallen woman at last!
EDGAR	'Ohhhhhh' (*they laugh*)
VIVIEN	Edgar?
EDGAR	Yes?
VIVIEN	You will see me after this weekend, won't you? I mean, you will call me?
EDGAR	Forever.
VIVIEN	Oh Edgar.
EDGAR	Yes?
VIVIEN	Let's have some wine.

EDGAR   On top of Whiskey Sours?

VIVIEN   Absolutely. Let's make tonight a celebration — of life and earth and us.

EDGAR   And your novel.

VIVIEN   Oh yes.

EDGAR   Red or white, what's your fancy?

VIVIEN   Who cares? Something grand but simple.

EDGAR   Elemental without being tawdry?

VIVIEN   Oh my, do you mind if I steal that?

EDGAR   I'd be flattered.

VIVIEN   Nurse Jane can exclaim it in a tornado! Are there tornadoes in Hawaii?

EDGAR   No.

VIVIEN turns away disappointed.

EDGAR   Tropical cyclones though.

VIVIEN   You're a Godsend!

EDGAR   They come with the trade winds — your basic Trade Wind Littoral Climate under the Koeppen Classification.

VIVIEN   And when they hit little Hawaii — look out!

EDGAR   Yes.

VIVIEN   Tell me more.

EDGAR   I'm not boring you?

VIVIEN   Lord, no! Go on, go on!

EDGAR   Well... (*beaming, then professorially*) ...we start with moist, warm air...

VIVIEN   Moist warm air.

EDGAR   Yes. In a low pressure area. With easy convection. Now a drop in this pressure — no matter how slight — starts the moist warm air circling or spinning...

VIVIEN   Or gyrating madly?

EDGAR   Exactly. Nice phrase.

VIVIEN   I use it a lot.

EDGAR   But as moisture condenses in the convection column, the updraft of air speeds up, gyrating even more madly.

VIVIEN   With passionate abandon?

EDGAR   Yes! And our air pressure lowers uniformly toward the vortex of our tropical cyclone. And how do we know our air pressure is lowering uniformly?

VIVIEN   How?

EDGAR   By observing the concentric pattern of isobars! (*in flight now*) And there's so much more to discover! The influence of jet streams, for example. Do tongues of polar air at high altitudes sweep south, pulling of dragging lower air with them as the axis turns, pressing northward? God, but it's a motherlode of intrigue to the initiated! But to the wine. 'Farewell, my love,' he said. 'I'm off to stalk the wine-cellar.' (*picking up the drink tray*)

VIVIEN   Hooray! Oh don't clear that. (*taking rye bottle*)

EDGAR   With wine?

VIVIEN   Of course not, silly. After. (*putting it under the couch*) Let's hide it under the ceremonial altar for a surprise nightcap. Like pirates and buried treasure (*whispering*) Shhh. X marks the spot.

EDGAR   Ahar, matie. (*lifting one leg in imitation of Long John Silver*) When I get back I'll give you all the dirt on Atmospheric Optics.

VIVIEN   Aloha. (*blowing him a kiss which he catches*)

EDGAR   Aloha. (*blowing her a kiss also which she catches, exiting with tray*)

***

Scene 38

"We'll Be Fine"

by Irene N. Watts

2 females

> This is a wonderful scene for two actors.
>
> Although the roles of Bridget and Mary are both mid-teens and should therefore not require as much character study as others in this section, the fact that they are both girls of another era, themselves strangers in a strange place, should provide more than enough challenge. These girls exist in a society with different values than today's world, as no doubt you will discover. Your audience will be as astonished, as you were, at the details of this world, if you are true to these characters and maintain your **focus**.
>
> Try to suggest the period, and **setting**, with the ideas provided in Watts' thoughtful **stage directions**. These will help communicate the feelings of Mary and Bridget. You can find a guy to play Patrick in the **flashback**, or you can simply omit it and go right to Bridget's next line, "He could charm the birds off the trees". Saying this line with a faraway, dreamy look in your eyes, *or* just the opposite, with a hardened, sarcastic **tone**, should help your portrayal of Bridget and give the audience a good picture of Patrick at the same time. Choose the **sub-text** you prefer.

We'll Be Fine

Characters MARY BARRETT, 16, a pregnant unwed mother. BRIDGET O'ROURKE, 15, a pregnant, unwed mother. PATRICK, 17, BRIDGET's boyfriend.

Alberta - late Sixties. A bedroom in Mrs. Grant's Rest Home for Ladies. A pseudonym for a place families sent pregnant teenagers in order to keep the family 'shame' private. These homes, many of which were run by religious orders, were spread all over Canada. The room is spotless though sparsely furnished. A hand-crocheted rug is placed in front of each of two single beds. A chest of drawers is centered between the beds. There is a small table by the window, and two upright chairs.

At rise, MARY kneels on the floor sorting out the top drawer of the chest. There is a knock on the door, soft. MARY gets to her feet clumsily. She is eight months pregnant.

MARY Come in.

She shuts the drawer. BRIDGET, a slight girl, stands in the doorway, holding a shabby suitcase.

BRIDGET Hello, Mrs. Grant said I was to come up. Is that OK with you?

MARY Of course. I'm Mary Barrett — make yourself at home. The bed nearest the door is yours, and you can have the bottom drawer of the chest.

BRIDGET I'm Bridget O'Rourke...

She holds out her hand timidly. MARY shakes it warmly.

...only, Mrs. Grant said not to use last names.

MARY Well, I won't tell. I'm going home soon — if this little fella will just get outta here. Never stops kicking. Hey, he's quiet for a minute, I'll take the chance and lie down.

She moves to her bed.

BRIDGET I'm sorry, I'm disturbing your rest.

MARY Don't be sorry, you don't have to be sorry about anything. I've made up my mind I'm not going to go through life apologizing for one mistake. If we had wedding rings, there'd be oohing and aahing and baby showers and good advice, instead of us being hidden away like lepers. So stop apologizing from now on.

BRIDGET I didn't mean...

MARY Oh, now I've scared you. It's just I've had a lot of time to think. I'm really glad to have someone to talk to again. My other roommate Liz — went home last week. Come on, why don't you get unpacked before supper?

BRIDGET Thanks, I will.

She hangs her hat and coat behind the door, and opens her suitcase, stowing her few possessions in the drawer.

I brought my knitting, I started a shawl.

MARY What a pretty color. You'll have plenty of time. We're free every afternoon, and after supper when we've done the dishes. Mrs. Grant is strict but fair. She lets us listen to

	the radio or watch TV sometimes. Makes sure we get a walk every day. Of course she comes with us to 'chaperone' meaning there's no chance to get a bus out of here, or make private phone calls, or write to anyone. We mustn't break 'cover'. The neighbors all know about us, but they don't stare when they see us out, speak a few words to Mrs. Grant sometimes and kinda look through us as if we don't exist.
BRIDGET	*(smiling and staring hard at MARY's huge waist)* That must be difficult.
	The girls laugh.
MARY	Glad to see you've kept a sense of humour.
BRIDGET	Mary, will you tell me what happens when babies are born? Do we get to keep them a while, before they get given to the new parents?
MARY	I don't think so. It's better not, they say, in case we get attached you know. They whisk them away to the nursery. But there's ways of sneaking a look, depends whose on duty. Liz, the girl who shared this room took hers home!
BRIDGET	You mean the father's going to marry her?
MARY	No, but her mother concocted this great story, she's told everyone her 'second cousin' died in childbirth, and so Lizzie went to help out, and she's bringing the baby back, because the family felt it was their duty to bring up the poor orphan. Can you imagine anyone believing her? She had a little boy, seven and a half pounds.

BRIDGET	I'm desperate to have a little girl, and if by some miracle I got to keep it, I'd sing to her and love her and take her side, no matter what.
MARY	You never know. How old are you? I'm sixteen.
BRIDGET	Fifteen.
MARY	Alyson, the girl in the next room, was seventeen. She went home empty-handed for the second time. There won't be a third one. She's been 'fixed'.
BRIDGET	You mean like an animal?
MARY	Yes. They said she was feeble minded. She wasn't, not very smart maybe, but nothing serious. She'll never have another baby.
BRIDGET	That's awful. Can they do that?
MARY	That's the law, they can do anything they like.[1]
BRIDGET	*(she starts to cry softly)* I've never heard of such an awful thing, what if...
	MARY gets up and puts an arm around BRIDGET.
MARY	I'm sorry, I shouldn't have told you. It won't happen to us. It doesn't happen often anymore. You and I will be fine.
	She goes to sit by the window.
BRIDGET	You sound like Patrick.
MARY	He's your boyfriend?

---

[1] The Alberta Sterilization Act. 1928 - 1972.

BRIDGET   Yes. That's what he always said, "You and me, colleen, we'll be fine." Five months and three days since the last time I saw him, and this is how fine I am.

MARY   Tell me about him.

BRIDGET   He's seventeen. We met back home in Kilkenny. We've been seeing each other for a year. Going for walks after church, or for a bit of a chat after school. He'd wait for me round the corner. So the nuns wouldn't catch us speaking. Terrible suspicious they are. Well they were right I suppose.

MARY   And then?

BRIDGET   The night before the family left for Dublin, the day before we were coming to Canada, there was a bit of a send off for us, food and dancing.

               Flashback. Piano under. BRIDGET leans against the wall. PATRICK enters.

PATRICK   I've been looking for you.

BRIDGET   I've been right here, where I said I'd be.

PATRICK   Can I get you a drink?

BRIDGET   Are you crazy, my Mother's watching.

PATRICK   Wish you weren't going. If you were older ... if I had work.

BRIDGET   We'll write often shall we?

PATRICK   As soon as I'm settled I'll let you know. I've a mind to go to Belfast, join up.

BRIDGET   You mean the military.

PATRICK   Why not? Money's regular and there's a chance to shoot the enemy.

BRIDGET   Oh Patrick, don't start talking about The Troubles tonight.

PATRICK   Come outside for a bit. There's a moon, that will make us both forget our troubles and the eyes that are watching us.

BRIDGET   Just for a short while then. It's cold.

PATRICK   You'll not feel the cold with my arm round you, colleen. You'll be fine.

PATRICK exits. End of flashback.

BRIDGET   He could charm the birds off the trees.

MARY   What did you do when you found out about the baby?

BRIDGET   I wrote him as soon as I was certain, but there was no answer. I don't know if he got any of my letters, and what could he do anyhow? But I wish I could have heard from him, just so I know he knows.

MARY   Yes. So then, you told your mother?

BRIDGET   I think she knew all along. I'd been awful sick right from the beginning. Coming over on the ship, I thought I was sea sick, and then when we arrived and it didn't get any better, my Mother said my system was all upset, I'd always been the delicate one. But it went on and on, and I couldn't keep my breakfast down, I'd get dizzy at work. I kept having to make excuses to sit down. I was on probation as a shoe clerk, and they sent me home, said I wasn't suitable. So I stayed home and helped with the others. I'm the oldest of five, I've three brothers younger than me, and a wee sister — four.

	Well one day last month I was hanging the wash on the line, and I saw my Mother watching me, the wind blowing my apron showing my stomach, too late to hide. That night after supper — liver and onions ...
MARY	Oh my God, you poor thing.
BRIDGET	I swear she cooked in on purpose to punish me. The kids were in bed, and my Father had gone off to the pub, I'd just finished the dishes. She pushed me down in the chair and held her crucifix to my lips and then made me hold it. "The truth now." she said. I never said a word, didn't need to, she said it for me. "It was that no-good Patrick O'Donovan, the night of the dance, wasn't it?" I nodded. No good denying it. She slapped me twice on each cheek and said, "That's for every month you've been carrying his bastard. Now get upstairs and stay in your room, I'm going to speak to Father Murphy." I stayed in the house for the next three days, she never spoke to me, and my Father never even looked at me and then I was told to pack my bag and here I am.
MARY	Well no one's going to slap you here.
BRIDGET	I wish I was older, I wish I had a job so I could keep my baby.
MARY	Don't give up, you can go to evening classes, finish your education, perhaps you can find a live-in job, get away from home for a while.
BRIDGET	*(knitting fiercely)* I'll make sure I get a good look at my baby, I'll ask the nurse to let me hold her, so I can tell her I hope she'll have a better life than mine.
MARY	Oh Bridget, our lives aren't over, they're just starting. We've made one mistake that's all.

BRIDGET	You're so sure of yourself, how do you manage it?
MARY	I'm not really, but I'm sure of one thing, I didn't want to marry the father of my baby, even though my Mother tried everything to make me change my mind.
BRIDGET	If I had the chance to marry Patrick.
MARY	But you see I don't love John—
BRIDGET	Well, why did you—
MARY	I don't really know. My brother introduced us. John's on the hockey team, a big hero. I guess I was flattered. There was a party, everyone was drinking. I wish it hadn't happened. You don't know how bad I feel about the baby, and I nearly gave in to my parents, it would be so much easier in a way. But it'd be two mistakes if I married someone I don't even like very much. It'll be hard going home, facing everyone. I messed up the first part of my life, but you know what Bridget, there's a lot left isn't there? I'll try and do better. (*beat*) The babies will go to good homes, won't they?
BRIDGET	Oh yes, I'm sure of it. Mary, thanks. No one's ever talked like this to me, like I'm a real person. Patrick's right, you're right. We'll be fine, and I pray to God the babies will be fine.

***

Scene 39

from "Dreaming and Duelling"

by John Lazarus and Joa Lazarus

2 males

SIDEKICK

    He is not Joel Goldner, a teenage nerd, but Valerian L'Estomber, 18th century noble, master of the sword, who, Zorro-like, rides to the rescue of revolutionary peasants. Get ze point?

    Joel's best friend, Eric, not to be left out of the fantasy, invents his own hero to ride alongside Valerian, and share in his daring exploits after first proving himself on a lonely road by moonlight to be as good a swordsman as the master.

    John Lazarus has an excellent ear for dialogue; his characters just *sound right*, and that's what makes him an outstanding writer. You should have no difficulty picturing the characters of Joel and Eric, and sharing the humour of this scene with the audience. And the sword-fight by moonlight is a bonus.

SIDEKICK

>*JOEL and ERIC are best friends, and, though "nerds" and outsiders, they are the stars of their high school's unusual course in fencing. After a particularly good practice session, JOEL has decided to let ERIC in on his private fantasy. The scene is JOEL's bedroom.*
>
>*JOEL and ERIC are looking through a cardboard carton, in and around which are items and papers about Valerian. ERIC is admiring a document on what looks like very old paper.*

JOEL   See, for the coat of arms, I used only the colours that they would use. This thing took me over a week.

ERIC   The paper looks so old.

JOEL   You singe it with a candle so it turns brown. Wait. Here. Looka this. This is his brooch, for keeping his scarf on.

ERIC   Where'd you get this? Is this real?

JOEL   Glass. Cost me a quarter at the Sally Ann. It was only a quarter because there's two of the diamonds missing, see? And they're missing because zey were removed by ze priests 'oo robbed hees grave.

ERIC   The priests robbed his grave!

JOEL   Oh, yes indeedy. Valerian was a sworn enemy of The Church.

ERIC   Okay, lemme get this straight: he was working on the side of the peasants, against The Church?

JOEL	Yeah, yeah, and against the nobility. Even his own family. The only guys who knew what a spy he was were three or four contacts among the revolutionary peasants. He was a legend in his own time.
ERIC	What was his name again?
JOEL	Valerian L'Estomber. It means Valerian drops. Eighteenth-century drug.
ERIC	"Valerian — Laisse-tomber", I get it. Dumb joke, Joel.
JOEL	This is not a joke, Eric, none of this is a joke.
ERIC	I had no idea you had any of this. You should write a book. You could make a book out of this.
JOEL	Nah.
ERIC	Oh, you should, man, you should! You got so many ideas about this guy, you could write a whole series!
JOEL	Writing some dumb series isn't the point.
ERIC	Joel, come on. You could make a fortune with this thing.
JOEL	It'd wreck it. It'd turn it into work. Besides, people wouldn't understand it. They'd think I was a total nut case. (*putting props back in box*)
ERIC	When Valerian did his spying — he didn't do it with anybody else?
JOEL	Nevaire.
ERIC	Wasn't there ever one guy who was like a longtime connection? Like a sidekick?

JOEL	Ay sidekeek? Valerian does not deal wit' ze sidekeek. 'E works always alone. Zere ees no one 'e can trost.
ERIC	Not even a peasant?
JOEL	What are you getting at?
ERIC	You know, like Sancho Panza. Like Tonto. A faithful companion.
JOEL	He has a dog named Marcel.
ERIC	A guy, a guy! A guy he can trust! Why are you being so dense?
JOEL	It just isn't his style.
ERIC	Aw, come on, Joel. What if somebody asked? To be his sidekick.
JOEL	Uh-uh.
ERIC	Some real smart peasant.
JOEL	He can fight off a hundred men single-handed. What's he need a sidekick for?
ERIC	Doesn't he ever need somebody to talk to? Just to talk to? He has all these terrible secrets stuffed into his head. Doesn't he ever get lonesome, Joel?
JOEL	(*brief pause*) He would have to be a great swordsman.
ERIC	Yeah, of course.
JOEL	Don't interrupt. Nerves of steel. Nerves of steel. And he would have to know the countryside like the back of his hand.

ERIC   He could be a, whaddaya call those guys. A highwayman! A highwayman! That's how he meets Valerian — he robs him. They have this fantastic swordfight. And Valerian knows a fantastic swordsman when he sees one, so he hires the guy.

JOEL   Cullen, that is simplistic.

ERIC   Why? Where's your imagination, Goldner? This is good! It's night time on the high road. And along comes Valerian on his horse, riding full throttle.

JOEL   (*pained*) Full throttle?

ERIC   Suddenly this guy jumps down on him from a cliff and knocks him off his horse and Valerian falls on his butt.

JOEL   No! Valerian always lands on his feet! Like a cat.

ERIC   Okay, but so does the other guy.

JOEL   Well, okay, maybe.

ERIC   Yeah, so he knocks Valerian off his horse and the horse runs away.

JOEL   Ze horse of Valerian does nevaire run away!

ERIC   Okay, so the horse sticks around. But his lantern goes out! (*turns off light — a home rheostat dial — and moonlight shines in through the window*) Valerian's lantern goes out! It's pitch, pitch black, they can't see each other at all!

JOEL   Okay — so — so they stand there on the highway. So?

ERIC   (*slow motion mime*) They draw their blades. (*they do so*) They salute.

They salute — ERIC's direct, JOEL's a figure-eight.

JOEL So how are they gonna fence each other, it's dark.

ERIC Uh — There! Ha! I can hear your footsteps. The highwayman lunges at the sound of the footsteps— (*lunging*)

JOEL And Valerian parries him. (*parries*) He parries him. 'Cause he heard the guy's blade swooshing through the air — no, wait, a blade doesn't swoosh on a forward lunge.

ERIC Yes it does! It does to these guys. Super sensitive hearing. Super sensitive hearing. Both of us.

They listen.

JOEL I can hear your breathing.

They listen.

ERIC I can hear yours.

JOEL So they fence.

Slow motion mimed fencing.

And then — Valerian the Cunning — holds his breath.

ERIC So does the other guy.

JOEL Aw come on, Eric. If they both hold their—

JOEL stops, listens.

ERIC Wha?

JOEL Sh!

ERIC	What?
JOEL	Sh! Sh sh sh.
	They listen, in awe.
	I can hear your heart beat. Eric, I can hear your goddamn heart beat.
	They listen.
ERIC	Not from there.
JOEL	Yes. Yes.
ERIC	*I* can't hear my—
JOEL	Sh!
	They listen.
ERIC	Yeah.
JOEL	Yeah.
ERIC	And yours. I can hear yours. Wow.
JOEL	Two hearts beating as one.
ERIC	The two greatest swordsman who ever lived on this whole planet.
JOEL	Yeah.
ERIC	Alone together.
JOEL	Yeah.
ERIC	In the pitch black night. On a road, somewhere in France.
JOEL	Destiny.
ERIC	So what do they do?

JOEL   They fence.

                Slow-motion mimed fencing.

                They fence all night long.

ERIC   Yeah.

JOEL   Not a word is spoken.

ERIC   Excellent.

JOEL   Just ze two 'arts beating — ze 'eavy breathing in 'armonee — ze boots scuffling on ze ground — ze slash and slice of ze blades.

ERIC   They miss each other by inches.

JOEL   Quarter of an inches.

ERIC   Eighth of an inches.

JOEL   Fantastique! All night long, peetch black, and nobody gets ze hit!

ERIC   And zen — wait a sec — (*goes and turns up the wall light*) Zen ze sky starts to get light in ze east.

JOEL   Yes. Yes. Ze sun starts comeeng op. We begin to see each othaire. Hold it, hold it. Perfect. Just the outlines at first.

ERIC   We slowly stop fencing.

JOEL   But of course. Because now eet ees too easee for us.

ERIC   And we get ze good look at each othaire.

JOEL   What's the highwayman look like?

ERIC   Uh — okay — he's wearing brown soft leather. Like, uh, like whatsit, calfskin.

JOEL	And a linen shirt? A rough old yellow shirt? With the neck open.
ERIC	Yeah, yeah. And one of those sort of Australian cowboy hats where they stick up one side and put a feather on it, you know? And a flower on his sleeve.
JOEL	He's sort of short and wiry. In his forties.
ERIC	Yeah, yeah, right, that's great. Also he has a grey moustache and, um, a ragged purple velvet eye patch.
JOEL	An eye patch? The, the guy is blind in one eye and he's a great swordsman?
ERIC	What the hey, why not?
JOEL	Well, depth perception, you need depth perception.
ERIC	Oh. Uh. Well. Uh, why'd ya think he had to develop super sensitive hearing!
JOEL	(*laughs*) Touché!
ERIC	Okay! What does Valerian look like?
JOEL	Very tall. Slendaire. Pale skeen, but healthy, yes? Green eyes, ze incradible green eyes. Ze long straight nose, ze black beard. I dressed een black and white, and buckles of silvaire, wit' lace on ze shirt.
ERIC	That's great. So we just look at each othaire for a while. And ze sun ees comeeng op.
	Turns light up further.
JOEL	(*bows*) Zees ees indeed an honaire. I am Le Comte Valerian L'Estomber.

ERIC	(*bows*) Compôte des Eglantiers. 'Ighwayman for ze Ravolution.
JOEL	Who des What?
ERIC	Compôte des Eglantiers. It's French for rose hip jam.
JOEL	(*brief pause*) Okay. Compôte — eef I may address you as, uh, Compôte — I greet you as a mastaire swordsman.
ERIC	Ah — Monsieur le Conte. Eet ees good to be appreciated.

They shake hands. Lights fade.

***

Les fondateurs des religions

Sébastien Doane

NOVALIS

Par un beau jour de printemps rue Verville

Chère Sara ce 9 juin 2013
L'auteur t'invite à poser un regard sur les religions & les cultures qui t'entourent tous les jours de ta vie.
grand-papa & grand-maman

Dans la collection *25 Questions junior*,

Les fondateurs des religions est publié par Novalis.

Révision : Lise Lachance

Mise en pages et couverture : Mardigrafe

© 2009, Les Éditions Novalis inc.

Novalis, 4475, rue Frontenac, Montréal (Québec) H2H 2S2
C.P. 990, succursale Delorimier, Montréal (Québec) H2H 2T1

Dépôts légaux : 1er trimestre 2009
                Bibliothèque nationale du Canada
                Bibliothèque nationale du Québec

Nous reconnaissons l'aide financière du gouvernement du Canada par l'entremise du Programme d'aide au développement de l'industrie de l'édition (PADIÉ) pour nos activités d'édition.

Cet ouvrage a été publié avec le soutien de la SODEC. Gouvernement du Québec — Programme de crédits d'impôt pour l'édition de livres — Gestion SODEC.

ISBN : 978-2-89646-096-0

Imprimé au Canada

Catalogage avant publication de Bibliothèque et Archives nationales du Québec et Bibliothèque et Archives Canada

Doane, Sébastien, 1978-

    Les fondateurs des religions

    (25 questions junior)

    Pour les jeunes.

    ISBN 978-2-89646-096-0

    1. Biographies religieuses - Miscellanées - Ouvrages pour la jeunesse. 2. Religions - Histoire - Miscellanées - Ouvrages pour la jeunesse. I. Titre. II. Collection: 25 questions junior.

BL72.D62 2009   j200.92'2   C2009-940509-1

Mot de l'auteur

Lorsque j'avais dix ans, je vivais dans un quartier dont la population était originaire de plusieurs pays. Je rencontrais souvent des personnes de cultures différentes en allant à l'école, au magasin ou au parc. Je leur posais toutes sortes de questions pour mieux les connaître.

Avec ce livre, je vous invite à découvrir ces cultures et ces religions qui nous entourent. Pour mieux les comprendre, nous répondrons aux 25 questions les plus courantes sur les fondateurs des grandes religions. Nous rencontrerons ainsi des hommes qui ont marqué l'histoire de l'humanité :

- Abraham, Moïse et David pour le judaïsme;
- Jésus le Christ, saint Paul et Martin Luther pour le christianisme;
- Muhammad, pour l'islam ou la religion musulmane;
- Siddhartha Gautama, le Bouddha, pour le bouddhisme;
- Guru Nanak, le fondateur du sikhisme.

Enfin, nous nous arrêterons à deux types de religions sans fondateur : les spiritualités amérindiennes et l'hindouisme.

Sous le nom de chacun d'entre eux, vous trouverez une **carte** et un **calendrier** pour préciser l'époque et le lieu où ils ont vécu.

Vous pourrez voir sur la ligne du temps qui suit l'ordre dans lequel ils sont entrés dans l'histoire du monde.

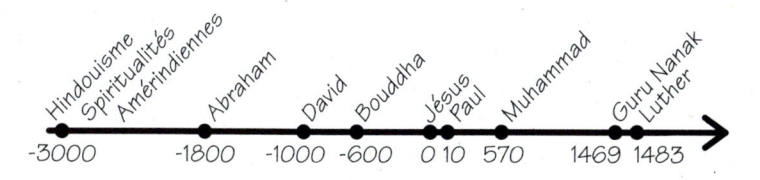

Hindouisme / Spiritualités Amérindiennes	Abraham	David	Bouddha	Jésus / Paul	Muhammad	Guru Nanak / Luther
-3000	-1800	-1000	-600	0 10	570	1469 1483

Bonne lecture et bonnes découvertes...

1

ABRAHAM

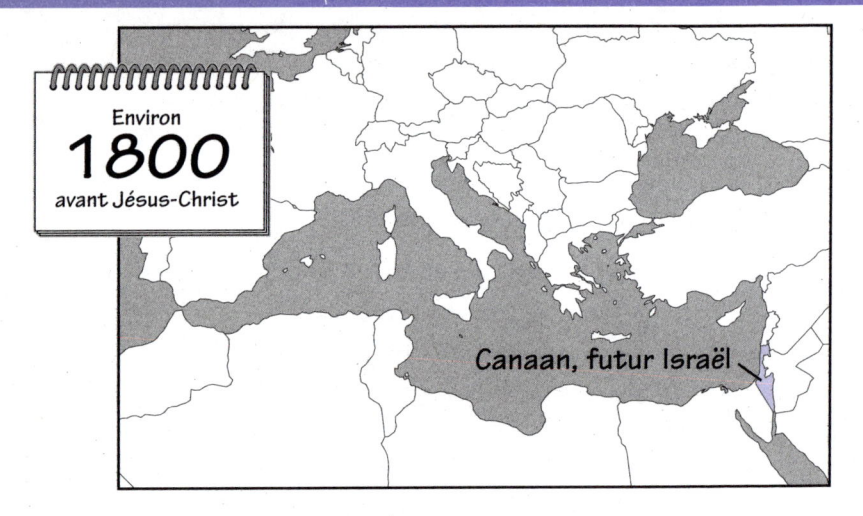

Environ **1800** avant Jésus-Christ

Canaan, futur Israël

Qui était Abraham ?

Voici l'histoire d'Abraham, le grand voyageur. Il a tout quitté pour répondre à l'appel de Dieu et faire alliance avec lui.

La première fois que Dieu s'adresse à Abraham, il lui demande de quitter son pays et sa famille pour aller vers un pays inconnu. Il lui promet de lui donner une terre et beaucoup d'enfants. Abraham part avec sa femme, Sarah, pour aller en Canaan, le pays que Dieu lui donne.

25 Questions junior Les fondateurs

Abraham et Sarah s'installent dans le nouveau pays, mais ils n'ont toujours pas d'enfant. Abraham est vieux et sa femme est stérile. Elle propose donc à son mari d'avoir un enfant avec sa servante, Hagar. Abraham et la servante ont un fils qu'ils nomment : « Ismaël », ce qui veut dire : « Dieu a entendu ma demande ».

Mais Dieu renouvelle sa promesse : Abraham et Sarah auront bien un enfant ensemble, malgré leur vieillesse. Les deux ne peuvent s'empêcher de rire : ils sont vraiment trop vieux ! Ils ont pourtant un fils qu'ils appellent : « Isaac », ce qui veut dire : « Que Dieu rie ».

Abraham a maintenant deux fils : Ismaël et Isaac. Sarah veut avoir toute l'attention d'Abraham pour elle et son fils. Elle demande alors à Abraham de chasser Hagar et Ismaël de la maison et il lui obéit. Dieu s'occupera de la servante et de son fils, qui iront vivre dans le désert.

Le récit le plus troublant dans l'histoire d'Abraham est celui de l'offrande de son fils en sacrifice. À cette époque, les gens trouvaient normal d'offrir à leur dieu ce qu'ils avaient de plus précieux : les meilleures récoltes ou de beaux animaux. En de rares occasions, ils sacrifiaient leurs propres enfants. Abraham croit que le moment est venu d'offrir à Dieu ce qu'il a de plus précieux : son fils Isaac. Il fait tous les préparatifs et emmène l'enfant sur une haute montagne. Au moment où il va tuer son fils, un ange arrête le bras d'Abraham. Il lui dit que Dieu a vu sa grande foi et qu'il n'a pas à faire ce sacrifice.

> Si tu veux lire l'histoire d'Abraham, trouve une Bible et va dans le premier livre, appelé Genèse, aux chapitres 11 à 25.

> En hébreu, le nom Abraham signifie : « père d'une multitude ». Dieu lui promet une grande famille. Il lui dit que sa descendance sera aussi nombreuse que les étoiles du ciel.

2

Pourquoi dit-on qu'Abraham est le père des juifs, des chrétiens et des musulmans ?

Abraham est considéré comme le père des trois grandes religions qui adorent un seul Dieu : le judaïsme, le christianisme et l'islam. La tradition juive a été la première à raconter son histoire dans le livre de la Genèse, le premier livre de la *Torah*. Les chrétiens ont gardé cette histoire dans la *Bible*, leur livre sacré. Pour eux, tous les livres de la tradition juive sont importants parce qu'ils permettent de mieux comprendre le Dieu dont Jésus a parlé.

Chez les musulmans, Abraham est aussi un prophète important. Son histoire est racontée dans le *Coran*, leur livre sacré, d'une façon un peu différente. En arabe, son nom est Ibrahim. Il est aussi appelé Khalil Allah, ce qui veut dire : « l'ami de Dieu ». Pour eux, il est le premier « musulman », c'est-à-dire : le premier à vouloir faire la volonté de Dieu de façon radicale.

- La Bible et le Coran racontent qu'Abraham a eu deux enfants : Ismaël et Isaac. Savais-tu que les musulmans se disent descendants d'Ismaël alors que les juifs ont Isaac comme ancêtre ? Juifs et musulmans auraient donc le même ancêtre : Abraham, le père des croyants.

- Aujourd'hui, même s'ils ont un ancêtre commun, les juifs et les musulmans se trouvent souvent en conflit. Il faut espérer qu'Abraham soit l'inspiration d'un vrai dialogue entre eux.

- Ensemble, juifs, chrétiens et musulmans représentent la moitié de la population de la planète, c'est-à-dire environ trois milliards d'habitants. Abraham est donc réellement le père d'une multitude !

3

MOÏSE

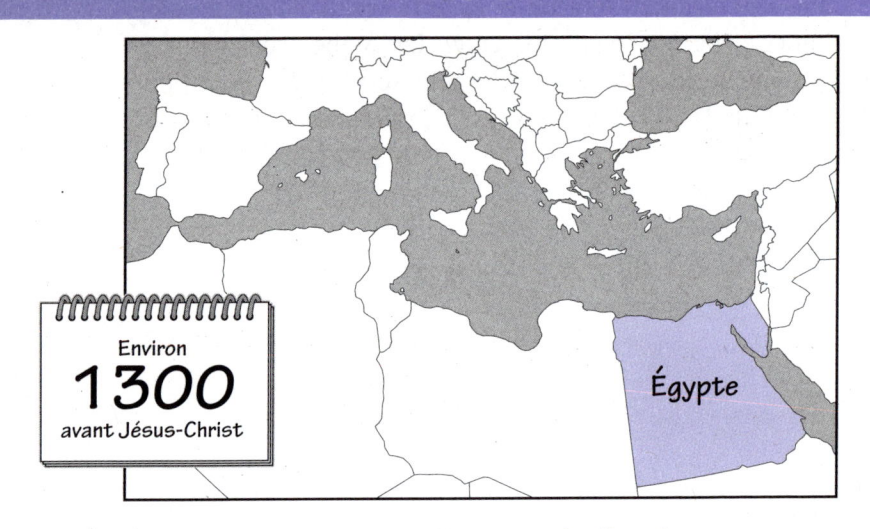

Environ **1300** avant Jésus-Christ

Égypte

Est-ce que Moïse est le fondateur de la religion juive ?

Les juifs d'aujourd'hui sont les descendants des Hébreux, dont Abraham est le père. L'histoire de ce peuple est racontée dans la *Torah*. Pourtant, Moïse est l'homme qui a le plus influencé la religion juive : il a été choisi par Dieu pour libérer son peuple de son esclavage en Égypte et il a reçu les dix commandements, signes de l'alliance entre Dieu et le peuple. Selon la tradition juive, il serait l'auteur de la *Torah*, le texte fondateur de cette religion. On peut donc dire que Moïse est bien l'un des fondateurs de la religion juive.

- La *Torah* est le texte le plus sacré de la religion juive. Il s'agit des cinq premiers livres de la Bible hébraïque : la Genèse, l'Exode, le Lévitique, le Livre des Nombres et le Deutéronome. Dans un sens large, le mot *Torah* désigne aussi l'ensemble de l'enseignement religieux juif, écrit et oral.

- La *Tanakh* ou Bible hébraïque contient en plus les écrits des prophètes et des sages : en tout, vingt-quatre livres écrits en hébreu, racontant l'histoire d'amour entre Dieu et son peuple.

- La *Torah* et la *Tanakh* se retrouvent dans la première partie de la Bible chrétienne appelée Ancien Testament.

4

Que veut dire le nom de Moïse ?

Moïse veut dire « sauvé des eaux ». Comme tout le peuple hébreu, les parents de Moïse étaient esclaves en

Égypte. Le Pharaon, roi d'Égypte, ordonna de tuer tous les garçons hébreux à leur naissance. Pour sauver son fils, la mère de Moïse fabriqua une corbeille flottante et la déposa dans les joncs, sur le bord du fleuve. Comme la fille du pharaon venait se baigner à cet endroit, elle entendit le bébé pleurer et elle eut pitié de lui. Elle savait bien que c'était un petit Hébreu, mais elle décida de l'élever comme son fils. Elle lui donne le nom de Moïse, « sauvé des eaux ».

Les noms dans la Bible ont presque toujours une signification importante en lien avec la vie ou la mission de la personne.

Pour lire l'histoire de la naissance de Moïse, va dans le deuxième livre de la Bible, l'Exode, au chapitre 2.

Peut-être as-tu déjà vu l'histoire de Moïse dans un film qui s'appelle *Le Prince d'Égypte*? C'est un film d'animation réalisé par la maison Dreamworks. Si ce fondateur t'intéresse, n'hésite pas à regarder ce film.

25 Questions junior Les fondateurs

5

Comment Moïse a-t-il rencontré Dieu ?

Moïse ne reste pas en Égypte toute sa vie. Une fois devenu adulte, il comprend qu'il est Hébreu et que son peuple est esclave. Un jour, il voit un Égyptien frapper un esclave hébreu. Sa réaction est de rendre coup pour coup et il tue l'Égyptien. Après ce meurtre, il doit s'enfuir et il va vivre avec des bergers.

Un jour qu'il faisait paître son troupeau sur une montagne appelée Horeb ou Sinaï, il se retrouve devant un buisson très particulier. Celui-ci est en flammes, mais il ne se consume pas, il reste vert. Il entend alors la voix de Dieu provenant du milieu du buisson : « Moïse ! Moïse ! Je suis le Dieu de ton père, d'Abraham, d'Isaac et de Jacob. J'ai vu la misère de mon peuple en Égypte. Je suis descendu pour le délivrer de la main des Égyptiens. Va maintenant ; je t'envoie vers Pharaon pour faire sortir d'Égypte, mon peuple. » La mission de Moïse est très claire : il doit libérer le peuple hébreu de son esclavage en Égypte.

Moïse demande alors à Dieu quel est son nom. Celui-ci répond : « *YHWH* ». Ces quatre lettres en hébreu se prononcent : *Yahvé*. On peut les traduire par : « Je suis qui je serai ». C'est un nom un peu énigmatique, mais il veut dire que Dieu sera avec Moïse et son peuple tout au long de son histoire. Ils le découvriront dans les actions qu'il accomplira en leur faveur.

25 Questions junior Les fondateurs

Il reste deux problèmes : les Hébreux ne croiront pas tout de suite que Moïse a rencontré Dieu et les Égyptiens ne laisseront pas partir facilement leurs esclaves. Pour rassurer son envoyé, Dieu lui donne le pouvoir d'accomplir des signes extraordinaires, comme changer de l'eau en sang ou un bâton en serpent. Il exercera ce pouvoir dans les dix plaies d'Égypte.

> Si tu veux en savoir plus, cette histoire se trouve dans la Bible, au livre de l'Exode, chapitres 3 et 4.

6

Moïse réussira-t-il à libérer son peuple ?

Après sa rencontre avec Dieu, Moïse retourne en Égypte. Il réunit les esclaves hébreux pour leur transmettre le message dont il est porteur. Puis, il s'adresse au Pharaon pour lui demander la libération de son peuple. Pharaon refuse, car il ne veut pas perdre ses travailleurs.

Commence alors une négociation difficile, au cours de laquelle Moïse doit utiliser les dons qu'il a reçus de Dieu.

Aussi longtemps que le Pharaon refusera de laisser partir les Hébreux, les malheurs s'abattront sur son pays. Ces catastrophes sont connues sous le nom de : « dix plaies d'Égypte ».

> Dans le langage de tous les jours, une plaie est une blessure. Mais, dans cette histoire, les plaies d'Égypte sont dix grandes catastrophes : invasion de sauterelles, grêle, morts de tous les premiers-nés, etc. Elles signalent la volonté inflexible de Dieu de libérer son peuple de l'esclavage.

Voici les dix plaies d'Égypte dans l'ordre où elles apparaissent dans la Bible :
1. les eaux du Nil, le principal fleuve du pays, se transforment en sang ;
2. des grenouilles envahissent les terres ;
3. des mouches et des moustiques s'attaquent aux gens ;
4. la vermine infeste le pays ;
5. une épidémie de peste se répand parmi les animaux ;
6. des furoncles (une maladie de la peau) apparaissent sur la peau des gens ;
7. la grêle détruit les récoltes ;
8. des sauterelles dévorent la végétation ;
9. l'obscurité règne pendant trois jours sur le pays ;
10. tous les premiers-nés des familles égyptiennes meurent durant la nuit.

Pharaon s'obstine et même après les plaies les plus terribles, il reste inflexible. Mais le dernier malheur, la mort des premiers-nés, est trop grand ! Il accepte enfin de laisser partir le peuple hébreu. Cependant, les esclaves sont à peine partis que Pharaon change d'idée ! Il lance son armée à la poursuite des Hébreux. Pour échapper à la poursuite des Égyptiens, Moïse et son peuple se dirigent tout droit vers la mer Rouge. Dieu ordonne à Moïse de prendre son bâton et d'ouvrir un passage au milieu des eaux. Les Hébreux traversent à pied sec. L'armée égyptienne croit pouvoir faire la même chose, mais Moïse étend alors son bâton et la mer se referme sur les chevaux et les cavaliers. Le peuple est sain et sauf de l'autre côté de la mer.

Cette histoire de la libération du peuple se trouve dans la Bible, aux chapitres 4 à 18 du livre de l'Exode.

Comment Moïse a-t-il reçu les dix commandements ?

Après la sortie d'Égypte, Moïse conduit le peuple à travers le désert vers la montagne du Sinaï. Il se souvient y avoir découvert Dieu, dans un buisson en flammes. Il laisse le peuple au pied de la montagne et monte à la rencontre de Dieu.

Dieu lui adresse alors les dix paroles que l'on appelle : les dix commandements :

1. « Je suis le Seigneur ton Dieu qui t'ai fait sortir du pays d'Égypte.
2. Tu n'auras pas d'autres dieux que moi.
3. Tu ne prononceras pas le nom de Dieu en vain.
4. Souviens-toi du jour du *sabbat*.
5. Honore ton père et ta mère.
6. Tu ne tueras point.
7. Tu ne commettras pas d'adultère (tromper son époux ou son épouse).
8. Tu ne voleras pas.
9. Tu ne feras pas de faux témoignages.
10. Tu ne voudras pas prendre ni la femme, ni la maison, ni rien de ce qui appartient à ton prochain. »

Ces dix lois sont inscrites sur des tables de pierre données par Dieu. En les respectant, le peuple manifestera qu'il est en alliance avec Dieu.

Pourtant, pendant que Moïse est sur la montagne, le peuple s'impatiente. Il décide de fabriquer la statue d'un veau avec l'or de tous ses bijoux. Puis il tourne autour en chantant et se prosterne pour l'adorer. Ce geste va clairement à l'encontre des deux premiers commandements de Dieu. Lorsque Moïse descend de la montagne et voit le spectacle, il se met en colère et brise les tables de pierre. Avant d'avoir existé, l'alliance entre Dieu et son peuple est déjà rompue. Puis, en réponse à la prière de Moïse, Dieu pardonnera à son peuple et lui donnera de nouvelles pierres sur lesquelles seront inscrits les dix commandements.

Ce récit montre la difficulté pour le peuple de faire entièrement confiance à un seul Dieu, alors que les autres nations en ont plusieurs. Il annonce aussi l'amour fidèle de Dieu pour un peuple qui lui, aura bien du mal à respecter les commandements, au cours de son histoire.

> Pour plusieurs sociétés, encore aujourd'hui, les dix commandements servent de règles de base dans la manière de vivre ensemble. C'est l'un des premiers codes de loi de l'histoire de l'humanité et il en a inspiré beaucoup d'autres. Des commandements similaires apparaîtront dans d'autres traditions religieuses et constitueront une sorte de règle d'or : « Ne fais pas aux autres ce que tu ne veux pas que l'on te fasse. »

Le sabbat est, pour les juifs, un jour de repos consacré au Seigneur. La Bible raconte que Dieu a pris six jours pour créer l'Univers et que le septième, il se reposa. Le sabbat commence le vendredi, au coucher du soleil, et se termine le samedi, à l'apparition de la première étoile. Le mot français « samedi » provient du mot « sabbat ».

Le récit du don des dix commandements apparaît deux fois dans la Bible : au livre de l'Exode, chapitres 19 à 34, et dans le Deutéronome, chapitres 5 à 10. En comparant les deux, on constate beaucoup de points de ressemblance. Les différences sont dues à deux manières de voir le même événement.

8

DAVID

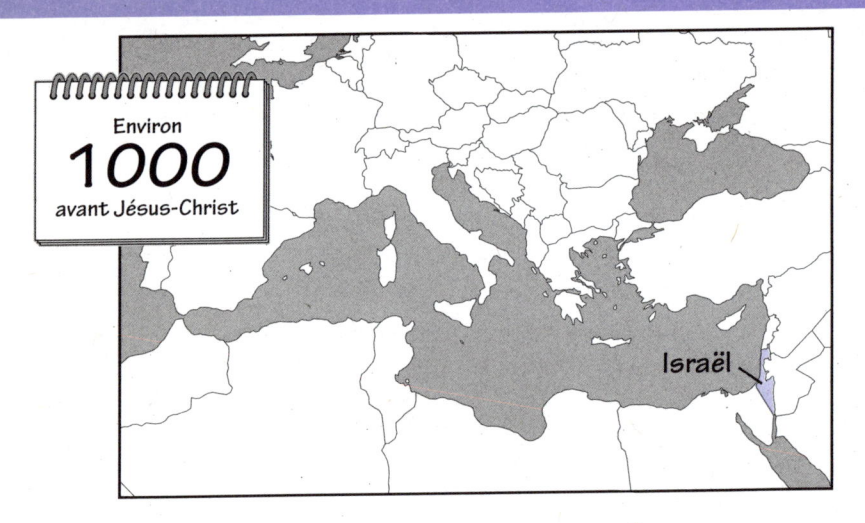

Environ
1000
avant Jésus-Christ

Israël

Quels sont les autres grands noms du judaïsme ?

En plus de Moïse, plusieurs personnages importants ont marqué l'histoire du judaïsme. Après la sortie d'Égypte et la traversée du désert, le peuple hébreu s'installe dans la Terre promise, le pays donné par Dieu. Peu à peu, il s'organise et manifeste le désir d'avoir un roi, comme les autres nations. Le plus grand roi de l'histoire d'Israël est David.

Sa vie est racontée dans les livres de Samuel, le premier livre des Rois et le livre des Chroniques.

David n'est encore qu'un petit berger quand il tue le géant Goliath avec son lance-pierre. Cet exploit permet au peuple d'Israël de remporter la victoire sur les ennemis philistins. Quand il devient roi, David soumet toutes les nations voisines. Un temps de prospérité et de paix s'ouvre alors pour son peuple. Il fait de Jérusalem la capitale de son royaume.

Le nom de David veut dire : « bien-aimé ». Ce grand roi est décrit comme un guerrier, mais aussi comme un musicien et un poète. Selon la tradition, il serait l'auteur de nombreux psaumes. Les psaumes sont à la fois des poèmes, des chants et des prières que l'on retrouve dans la Bible.

Un autre roi important s'appelle Salomon. C'est l'un des fils de David. Il a construit le premier temple de Jérusalem. On dit qu'il était d'une sagesse étonnante. Plusieurs livres de la Bible se réclament de lui.

La religion juive compte aussi d'importants prophètes. Ils avaient pour mission de transmettre la parole de Dieu au peuple. Pour connaître leur histoire et leurs enseignements, il suffit de lire leurs livres que l'on trouve dans la Bible. Ils portent les noms d'Isaïe, Jérémie, Ézéchiel, Daniel, Osée, Joël,

Amos, Abdias, Jonas, Michée, Nahoum, Habaquq, Sophonie, Aggée, Zacharie et Malachie.

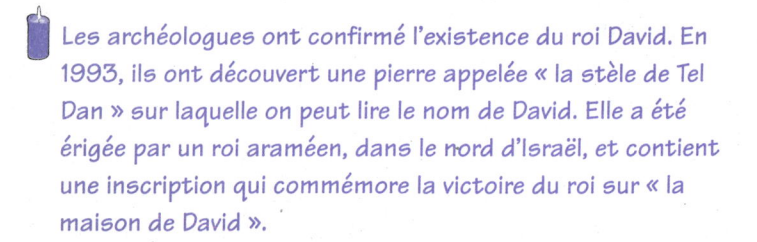

> Jérusalem est encore la capitale d'Israël. Elle est une ville sainte pour les juifs, les chrétiens et les musulmans.

> Les archéologues ont confirmé l'existence du roi David. En 1993, ils ont découvert une pierre appelée « la stèle de Tel Dan » sur laquelle on peut lire le nom de David. Elle a été érigée par un roi araméen, dans le nord d'Israël, et contient une inscription qui commémore la victoire du roi sur « la maison de David ».

9

JÉSUS DE NAZARETH

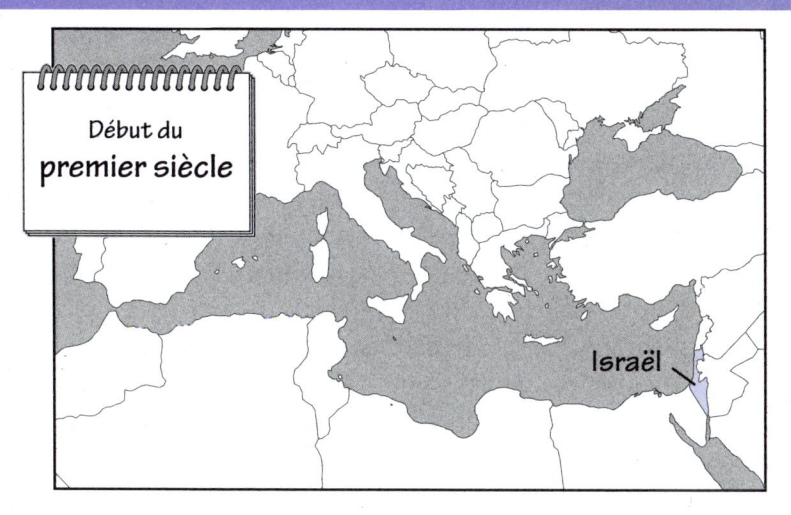

Début du **premier siècle**

Israël

Pourquoi fête-t-on la naissance de Jésus à Noël ?

C'est la coutume de s'offrir des cadeaux à Noël. Le père Noël vient faire un tour dans nos rues, on a congé d'école, on décore l'arbre de Noël, on visite la famille. À travers toutes ces activités amusantes, il est facile d'oublier le vrai sens de la fête de Noël.

Le mot « Noël » vient du latin et signifie : « jour de la naissance ». Il s'agit de la naissance de Jésus. On en fait une fête, comme ton anniversaire. La messe célébrée ce soir-là permet à tous les chrétiens de se rappeler les événements mystérieux qui ont entouré cette naissance.

L'évangile de Luc raconte qu'à cette époque l'empereur voulut savoir combien d'habitants vivaient en Israël. Chacun devait donc aller s'inscrire dans la ville où il était né. Marie, enceinte, part pour Bethléem, avec son mari, Joseph. À leur arrivée, ils constatent qu'il ne reste plus aucune chambre à louer. Pourtant, le moment d'accoucher est arrivé pour Marie. Ils se réfugient dans une étable et Marie donne naissance à son fils qu'elle couche dans une mangeoire pour animaux. Les bergers des alentours sont avertis par des anges de la naissance d'un Sauveur. Ils sont les premiers à venir adorer l'enfant. Cette naissance dans une étable nous montre que Dieu se fait proche des pauvres et des petits. Il aurait pu choisir des façons grandioses de se faire connaître, mais il a préféré le faire par un petit bébé, né dans la pauvreté.

Une autre version de cette histoire est présentée au début de l'évangile de Matthieu. On y retrouve les mages, des sages d'Orient, qui viennent adorer « le roi des Juifs ». Ils ont fait le voyage en suivant une étoile. Ils demandent au roi Hérode de les informer du lieu de la naissance. Mais celui-ci prend peur : risque-t-il de perdre son pouvoir ? Pour se protéger, il fait tuer tous les enfants de moins de deux ans. Averti dans un rêve, Joseph décide d'emmener sa petite famille en Égypte. Quelques années plus tard, après la mort d'Hérode, ils viendront habiter à Nazareth.

Le mot « crèche » vient d'un mot latin qui signifie : « mangeoire ». C'est saint François d'Assise qui a créé, en 1223, la première crèche vivante, en utilisant des personnages réels joués par les gens du village. Même les animaux étaient vivants ! Depuis, on trouve des crèches dans tous les pays chrétiens et elles sont faites avec des figurines de cire, de plâtre, de bois, de paille, etc.

Savais-tu que le 25 décembre n'est pas la date exacte de la naissance de Jésus ? Personne ne connaît cette date. La fête de Noël a été fixée plus de trois cents ans après la mort de Jésus. Les chrétiens ont choisi ce jour, où les Romains célébraient la fête de la lumière, pour dire que Jésus était « la lumière du monde ». Si tu fais attention, tu verras qu'à partir du 25 décembre les journées commencent à rallonger et les nuits à raccourcir.

Le nom de Jésus se prononçait « Yéshoua », en araméen, sa langue maternelle. Il veut dire : « Dieu sauve ».

Pourquoi parle-t-on encore de Jésus aujourd'hui?

Les sources d'information les plus sûres sur Jésus sont les évangiles. Ces quatre livres ont été écrits par des auteurs que l'on connaît sous les noms de Matthieu, Marc, Luc et Jean. En lisant ces récits, on peut mieux comprendre pourquoi on parle encore de Jésus aujourd'hui, deux mille ans après sa mort.

Jésus était un juif et il voulait enseigner une façon plus personnelle de prier Dieu. Lorsqu'il parle de Dieu, il utilise le mot « papa », pour dire à quel point Dieu nous aime. C'était nouveau car, à cette époque, on le voyait plutôt comme quelqu'un de distant. Tout l'enseignement de Jésus pourrait se résumer dans cette phrase : « Aime Dieu et aime ton prochain comme toi-même. »

Jésus ne fait pas que de beaux discours, il accomplit des actions concrètes pour renforcer ce qu'il dit. À plusieurs reprises, il guérit des malades et il prend le parti des pauvres, des étrangers, des prostituées et de tous ceux et celles qui sont rejetés par la société.

Autour de lui, les gens réagissent de différentes façons : plusieurs sont vraiment touchés et acceptent de devenir ses disciples, d'autres restent indécis ou indifférents. Son message et ses actions provoquent l'hostilité des autorités en place. Comme elles se sentent menacées, elles vont même jusqu'à arrêter Jésus et à le faire mourir sur une croix.

Après la mort de Jésus, ses disciples annoncent sa résurrection et affirment qu'il est le Messie. Ils répandent son histoire et ses enseignements. Des personnes de différentes origines se joignent à eux pour former des communautés qui donneront naissance à la religion chrétienne. Voilà pourquoi on parle encore de Jésus, deux mille ans plus tard.

Qu'est-ce que le Messie ?

Le mot « Messie » existait déjà pour les juifs. Le Messie est l'envoyé de Dieu attendu par le peuple juif. Cet envoyé devait répondre à tous les espoirs, toutes les attentes du peuple. En Jésus, les premiers chrétiens reconnaissent le Sauveur promis par Dieu. En grec, on traduit par le mot « Christ », c'est pourquoi Jésus est souvent appelé : « Jésus-Christ ».

Pourquoi Jésus a-t-il fait des miracles ?

Lorsqu'on lit les évangiles, on voit Jésus accomplir des gestes peu ordinaires. Il guérit des malades, transforme de l'eau en vin, multiplie des pains et des poissons, calme une tempête, marche sur l'eau et même redonne la vie à son ami Lazare qui vient de mourir. Ces événements nous paraissent bizarres. On n'en voit pas dans la vie de tous les jours.

Ces miracles nous posent une question : qui est-il, ce Jésus, capable de tels gestes ? Les récits de miracles sont une façon de dire que Jésus n'était pas un homme comme les autres. Il était perçu comme quelqu'un d'exceptionnel par son entourage, à cause de l'intensité de sa relation avec Dieu. Cet amour le rendait assez fort pour accomplir des actions étonnantes.

L'important n'est pas de savoir s'ils sont historiques, mais plutôt de découvrir ce qu'ils veulent nous enseigner. Pourquoi a-t-il fait cela ? Que voulait-il nous dire ?

Les miracles accomplis par Jésus doivent être vus comme des signes qui parlent de Dieu. Quand Jésus nourrit la foule, il révèle un Dieu qui nourrit ceux qui ont faim. Quand il guérit des malades, il annonce un Dieu qui s'occupe des malheureux. Quand il calme la tempête, on comprend que la création lui obéit comme à l'envoyé de Dieu. En redonnant la vie à son ami Lazare, il montre que la vie voulue par Dieu est plus forte que la mort. Les miracles sont donc des signes du royaume de Dieu, là où il n'y aura plus de faim, de maladie et même de mort.

Les capacités de Jésus sont différentes des nôtres. Il a des habiletés que nous n'avons pas. Il savait comment aider les gens exclus ou blessés. Il pouvait guérir les cœurs et les corps.

- La Bible est une vraie bibliothèque. Elle est composée de 73 livres. Elle est divisée en deux parties : l'Ancien Testament et le Nouveau Testament.

- Pourquoi dit-on : « Testament » ? Le mot vient du latin et peut être traduit par : « alliance ». L'Ancien et le Nouveau Testament parlent donc de l'alliance entre Dieu et ceux et celles qui croient en lui.

- L'Ancien Testament regroupe les textes sacrés des juifs croyants. Ils sont lus aussi par les chrétiens.

- Le Nouveau Testament rassemble des écrits des premiers chrétiens. On y retrouve entre autres les évangiles, qui racontent la vie de Jésus.

Que veut-on dire quand on affirme que Jésus est ressuscité ?

Les chefs religieux et politiques décident d'arrêter Jésus et de le condamner à mort. Quand les soldats se présentent, tous les disciples l'abandonnent. Ils ont trop peur de ce qui pourrait leur arriver. Jésus meurt sur une croix et on pourrait penser que toute cette histoire est finie ! En réalité, elle ne fait que commencer.

Des femmes vont au tombeau pour parfumer le corps de Jésus, mais elles le trouvent complètement vide. Elles comprennent alors que Jésus est ressuscité, c'est-à-dire qu'il est revenu à la vie. Les évangiles racontent plusieurs apparitions de Jésus ressuscité aux disciples.

Comment comprendre cette résurrection ? Jésus qui était mort est revenu à la vie. Mais ce n'est pas un retour à la vie d'avant. La preuve ? Chaque fois qu'il se montre à des gens qui l'ont bien connu, ils ne le reconnaissent pas tout de suite. Jésus est bien vivant, mais d'une vie nouvelle, sur laquelle la mort n'aura pas de prise.

Après leur rencontre avec le Ressuscité, les disciples, qui avaient peur et se cachaient, sortent au grand jour. Ils ont une bonne nouvelle à annoncer : Jésus a été ressuscité par Dieu et il fera la même chose pour tous ceux et celles qui croiront que Jésus était son envoyé ! Depuis ce jour, les chrétiens célèbrent à Pâques la mort et la résurrection de Jésus.

> Comment faut-il écrire le mot : Pâque ou Pâques ? Pâque (sans s final) désigne la fête juive de la sortie d'Égypte. En hébreu, le mot signifie : « passage » et rappelle le passage à travers la mer Rouge et le désert. La mort et la résurrection de Jésus ont eu lieu au cours de la célébration juive de la Pâque. C'est pourquoi les chrétiens ont conservé le même mot, en ajoutant un « s » à la fin : Pâques. On parle alors du passage de Jésus de la mort à la vie.

13

Pourquoi les chrétiens disent-ils que Jésus est à la fois homme et Dieu ?

Les premiers disciples ont rencontré un homme en chair et en os, mais qui parlait d'une façon nouvelle et qui accomplissait des gestes extraordinaires. Ce n'est qu'après sa mort et sa résurrection qu'ils ont vraiment compris que Jésus avait en lui quelque chose de divin.

25 Questions junior Les fondateurs

Ils l'ont donc révélé à tout le monde comme le Messie, l'envoyé de Dieu et même le Fils de Dieu.

Dans l'évangile, Jésus demande à ses disciples : « Qui dites-vous que je suis ? » Les disciples disent d'abord que la plupart des gens croient qu'il est un prophète. Puis, Pierre affirme : « Tu es le Christ (Messie), le Fils du Dieu vivant ! » (Évangile de Matthieu, chapitre 16).

Avec le temps, les chrétiens en arrivent à voir Jésus à la fois comme un homme et comme un Dieu. Encore aujourd'hui, chacun peut se demander : qui est Jésus ? Pour certains, c'est un homme comme les autres ; pour les juifs et les musulmans, c'est un grand prophète, porteur d'un message de Dieu. Mais pour les chrétiens, il n'est pas seulement un prophète, il est le Messie, l'envoyé de Dieu qui nous donne une vie éternelle.

Qui est Jésus ? Pose la question à ta famille et à tes amis. Tu verras que chacun a une façon différente de parler de lui. Et toi, qu'en penses-tu, qui est Jésus, selon toi ?

PAUL DE TARSE

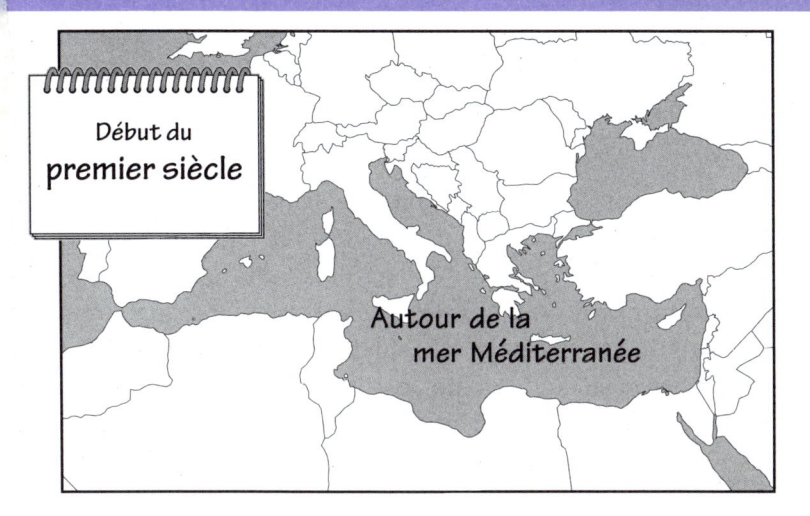

Début du **premier siècle**

Autour de la mer Méditerranée

Qui est Paul de Tarse ? Comment a-t-il aidé le christianisme à grandir ?

Après la résurrection de Jésus, les premiers chrétiens se rassemblent dans des petites communautés pour vivre leur foi. L'un des fondateurs de ces communautés est Paul de Tarse.

Avant de devenir lui-même chrétien, Paul les pourchassait et voulait leur mort à tous. Puis, un jour, il a fait l'expérience de la rencontre de Jésus ressuscité. Devant une forte lumière, Paul tombe par terre et entend la voix de Jésus lui demandant pourquoi il le persécutait ! Paul a compris qu'il devait changer de vie. Il s'est empressé d'annoncer partout autour de lui qu'il avait rencontré Jésus, le Vivant. Il deviendra l'un des apôtres les plus importants du christianisme.

La bonne nouvelle que Paul annonce tient en peu de mots : Jésus est ressuscité et nous aussi nous ressusciterons, grâce à lui. Il voyagera partout, autour de la mer Méditerranée, pour former des communautés qui se rassembleront au nom de Jésus. C'est pourquoi on appelle Paul : « l'apôtre des nations ». Avant qu'il commence sa mission, les chrétiens étaient majoritairement d'anciens juifs qui avaient adopté le message de Jésus. Pour Paul, ce message doit rejoindre tout le monde, il est universel. Hommes ou femmes, esclaves ou maîtres, juifs ou non juifs, tous peuvent devenir disciples de Jésus, c'est-à-dire chrétiens.

Pour rester en contact avec les communautés qu'il a fondées, Paul leur écrit des lettres. On les retrouve dans le Nouveau Testament. Elles parlent des aspects concrets de la vie chrétienne. Elles expliquent comment comprendre la foi en Jésus Christ. Encore aujourd'hui, à la messe, les chrétiens relisent ces lettres, que Paul a écrites il y a deux mille ans.

Paul est originaire de la ville de Tarse. C'est pourquoi nous l'appelons Paul de Tarse. À l'époque, c'était une ville importante à cause de son port. Aujourd'hui, Tarse fait partie de la Turquie.

On l'appelle aussi saint Paul. Sais-tu ce qu'est un saint ? Les saints et les saintes sont des personnes qui ont vécu une vie exemplaire. Pour nous, ils sont comme des images de Dieu. Tous les chrétiens sont appelés à devenir des saints, en vivant le mieux possible. Tu peux donc devenir un saint ou une sainte, toi aussi !

Le mot « apôtre » veut dire : « envoyé », en grec. Au sens large, il s'applique aux premiers chrétiens qui vont partout pour parler de la résurrection de Jésus. Au sens étroit, il désigne les douze hommes choisis par Jésus pour l'accompagner pendant sa vie ; ils sont appelés : « les douze apôtres ». Paul ne fait pas partie du groupe des Douze, mais il se présente quand même comme le plus petit des Apôtres, parce qu'il vu Jésus ressuscité.

Les premiers chrétiens seront persécutés pour leur foi. D'abord les Juifs, puis les Romains ne supporteront pas ces croyants d'une nouvelle religion. Les femmes et les hommes qui meurent pour leur foi sont appelés : « martyrs ». Ils sont considérés comme des saints dès leur mort.

25 Questions junior Les fondateurs

15

MARTIN LUTHER

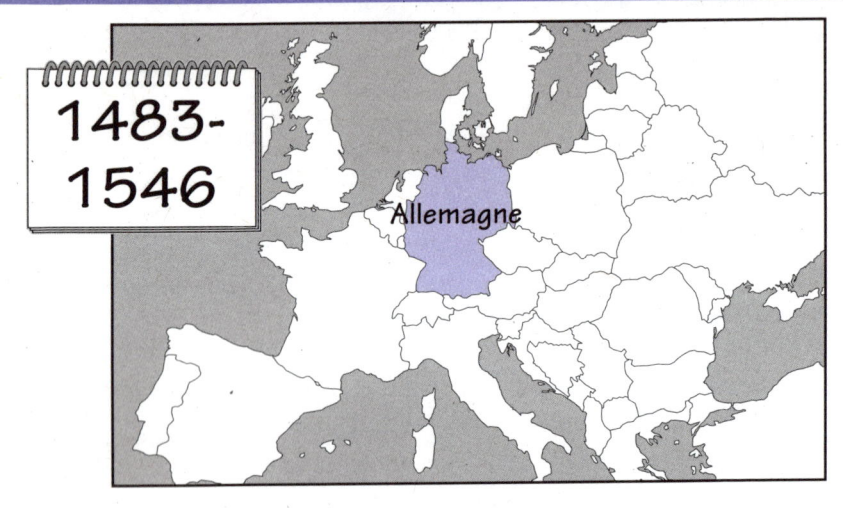

1483-1546

Allemagne

Tous les chrétiens sont-ils catholiques ? Qui est Martin Luther ?

Pendant deux mille ans, il y a eu différentes façons de comprendre et de vivre la foi en Jésus. Beaucoup de groupes se sont formés pour vivre leur foi chrétienne à leur manière. C'est pourquoi on trouve des catholiques, des orthodoxes, des anglicans et différents types de protestants. Martin Luther est l'un des fondateurs de la tradition protestante.

Martin Luther était un moine catholique pour qui la Bible était très importante. Il la lisait, en se posant toutes sortes de questions, dont une en particulier : qu'est-ce qui nous sauve ? Qu'est-ce qui fera qu'après la mort, j'irai au paradis plutôt qu'en enfer ? En lisant les lettres de saint Paul, il est devenu convaincu que seul Dieu sauve et qu'il le fait gratuitement. Il comprend alors que ce ne sont pas les bonnes actions qui rendent les gens agréables aux yeux de Dieu, mais la foi en Jésus sauveur. Pour vivre éternellement, les chrétiens doivent accepter la vie nouvelle donnée par Dieu.

Luther trouve que l'Église de son temps ne vit pas comme Jésus l'avait demandé. Il propose donc de nouvelles façons de voir la foi chrétienne. Après de longues discussions, cette prise de position est rejetée par le pape Léon X. Martin Luther se voit condamné par l'Église catholique. Pourtant, ses idées sont très populaires en Allemagne et plusieurs chrétiens se joindront à lui. Ils deviendront les premiers protestants.

Luther voit dans la Bible la seule source de connaissances sur Dieu. À l'époque, le livre n'existait qu'en latin, une langue mal comprise par les gens du peuple ; seuls les prêtres avaient donc accès à la parole de Dieu. Martin Luther la traduira en allemand, la langue de son pays. Depuis, tous les protestants sont encouragés à lire la Bible par eux-mêmes.

- Il ne faut pas confondre Martin Luther, le fondateur du protestantisme, qui a vécu en Allemagne au 15e siècle, et Martin Luther King, le défenseur des droits des Noirs. Celui-là était un pasteur américain et il a vécu au 20e siècle. Le prénom de Martin Luther lui a été donné en mémoire du fondateur du protestantisme.

- Martin Luther était moine. Les moines sont des hommes qui ont choisi de vivre en communauté dans un monastère. Ils consacrent beaucoup de temps à la prière, à l'étude et au silence pour rencontrer Dieu. Les femmes aussi peuvent vivre cette expérience, on les appelle moniales.

- Il y a deux façons de comprendre le mot « protestant ». Pour certains, il s'agissait de protester contre la dégradation de la foi dans l'Église catholique. En réalité, ce mot vient du latin *pro testare* et signifie « témoigner de sa foi ». Les protestants se présentent donc comme ceux qui témoignent de leur foi.

MUHAMMAD

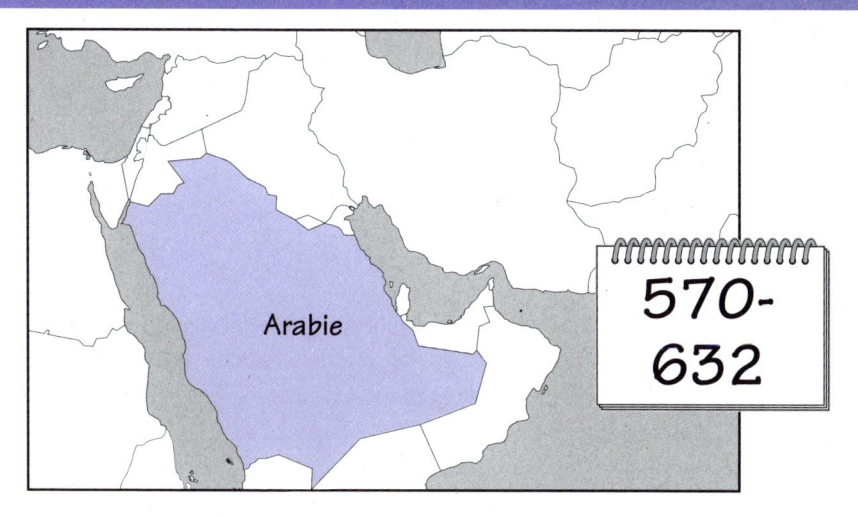

570-632

Qui est le fondateur de l'islam ?

Muhammad est le prophète et le fondateur de l'islam. Son nom est parfois traduit par « Mahomet » ou « Mohamed ». De nombreux autres noms lui ont été attribués : le messager, l'envoyé, l'élu, etc.

Il est né en 570 à La Mecque, dans le désert d'Arabie. Il fait partie de la tribu de Quraych, qui se présente comme celle des descendants d'Ismaël, le premier fils d'Abraham.

Cette tribu avait la garde de la *Ka'ba*, un sanctuaire important où chaque nation venait déposer des idoles représentant ses dieux.

Savez-vous comment prononcer Muhammad ? Le son de la lettre arabe traduit par « ha » n'existe pas vraiment en français. On pourrait dire que c'est comme faire un « h » mais profondément dans la gorge. On pourrait dire que son nom se prononce : Mouhhhammad.

Aujourd'hui, la Ka'ba est un grand cube noir placé au centre de la mosquée (le lieu de rassemblement des musulmans) de La Mecque. Elle ne contient plus d'idoles et elle est recouverte d'un tissu sur lequel ont été brodés des versets du Coran. Les musulmans du monde entier se tournent vers la Ka'ba lorsqu'ils prient. Chacun est encouragé à y venir en pèlerinage, au moins une fois dans sa vie.

Comment Allah (Dieu) a-t-il fait de Muhammad son messager ?

Allah est le nom du Dieu de l'islam. En arabe, Allah signifie : « le Dieu ». Pour les musulmans, seul Allah est Dieu. Il est le créateur de toutes choses. Ils lui donnent quatre-vingt-dix-neuf noms, pour tenter de le décrire : Allah le protecteur, Allah le juste, Allah le créateur, etc.

Selon la tradition, Muhammad se rendait souvent dans une grotte pour se recueillir. C'est là qu'à l'âge de 40 ans, il aurait vu pour la première fois l'ange Gabriel chargé de lui transmettre la parole d'Allah. Pendant vingt-trois ans, Muhammad recevra cette révélation qu'il transmettra à ses proches. Une vingtaine d'années après sa mort, ces révélations seront mises par écrit. Elles constituent le Coran qui veut dire : « récitations ».

Effrayé par l'apparition de l'ange, Muhammad se réfugie auprès de sa femme, Khadijah, et lui raconte ce qui vient d'arriver. Tout de suite, elle croit que son époux est le prophète attendu et lui apportera un soutien indéfectible. Elle est considérée comme la première croyante. Muhammad fonde un groupe qui s'appelle : « les musulmans », ce qui veut dire : « ceux qui se soumettent à la volonté d'Allah ». Puis, son enseignement devient public et s'étend à l'ensemble de sa tribu.

25 Questions junior Les fondateurs

Pour les habitants de La Mecque, son message est difficile à entendre. Il demande de renoncer aux multiples dieux qu'ils adorent et beaucoup s'y refusent. Pourtant, Muhammad réussit à constituer un cercle de disciples qui, au bout de cinq ans, en compte une centaine. La croissance rapide du nombre de musulmans inquiète les Mecquois. Ils déclencheront des persécutions contre Muhammad et les siens. Le prophète conclut alors un pacte avec des croyants de la ville de Médine et les musulmans de La Mecque pour aller vivre là-bas, en 622. C'est ce que l'on appelle « l'hégire ».

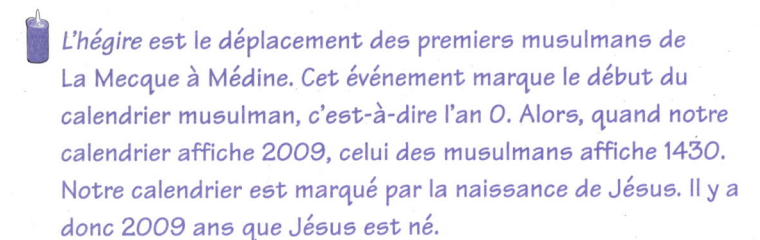

L'hégire est le déplacement des premiers musulmans de La Mecque à Médine. Cet événement marque le début du calendrier musulman, c'est-à-dire l'an 0. Alors, quand notre calendrier affiche 2009, celui des musulmans affiche 1430. Notre calendrier est marqué par la naissance de Jésus. Il y a donc 2009 ans que Jésus est né.

Savais-tu que Gabriel, l'ange qui rapporte les paroles d'Allah à Muhammad, joue aussi un rôle important chez les juifs et les chrétiens ? Dans la Bible, c'est lui qui annonce à Marie qu'elle sera mère de Jésus.

Comment se termine la vie de Muhammad ?

Lorsqu'il arrive à Médine, Muhammad est tout à la fois chef religieux, chef politique et chef militaire de son groupe. Il fait alliance avec les deux tribus arabes et les trois tribus juives qui vivent à Médine.

L'armée musulmane est attaquée par les Mecquois et riposte. Plusieurs batailles ont lieu entre les deux villes. Finalement, Muhammad marche vers La Mecque avec des milliers de soldats. La ville se rend sans combattre et les habitants de La Mecque deviennent eux aussi des « musulmans ». Bientôt, c'est presque toute l'Arabie qui embrasse l'islam. Muhammad unifie les diverses tribus arabes et envoie des ambassadeurs dans les empires voisins pour transmettre son message.

Après avoir organisé le fonctionnement de l'islam à La Mecque, Muhammad retourne à Médine, où il meurt le 8 juin 632, à l'âge de 63 ans.

La vie de Muhammad est donc très différente de celle des autres fondateurs de grandes religions, Jésus ou le Bouddha, par exemple. Ceux-ci n'ont pas cherché à devenir des chefs politiques et militaires.

Pourquoi ne voit-on pas d'images de Muhammad ou très rarement ?

L'islam se divise en deux grandes familles : les chiites et les sunnites. Pour les sunnites, il est interdit de dessiner, peindre, photographier tout être possédant une âme. C'est ce qui explique que l'on ne retrouve pas d'images du prophète Muhammad. Toute représentation serait considérée comme un blasphème. Toutefois, cette règle n'est pas respectée de façon absolue : Muhammad apparaît parfois chez les Persans et les Turcs, mais la forme du visage est laissée vide ou elle est cachée par un voile ou une flamme.

- Tout l'art arabe est marqué par cette interdiction de représentation. Il a développé une façon incroyablement riche d'écrire les versets du Coran. Les motifs sur les tapis ou les vases sont donc souvent des passages du Coran, dans une calligraphie d'une beauté exceptionnelle.

- Dans les dix commandements de la Bible, on retrouve l'interdiction de la fabrication des idoles (les images de dieux). Certains groupes de chrétiens ont donc choisi de ne pas faire de représentations de Dieu ou de Jésus. Par exemple, les croix protestantes ne portent pas le corps de Jésus. D'autres chrétiens, au contraire, aiment utiliser les images pour enseigner les récits bibliques. Selon eux, puisque Jésus était un homme, on peut le représenter.

20

LE BOUDDHA (SIDDHARTHA GAUTAMA)

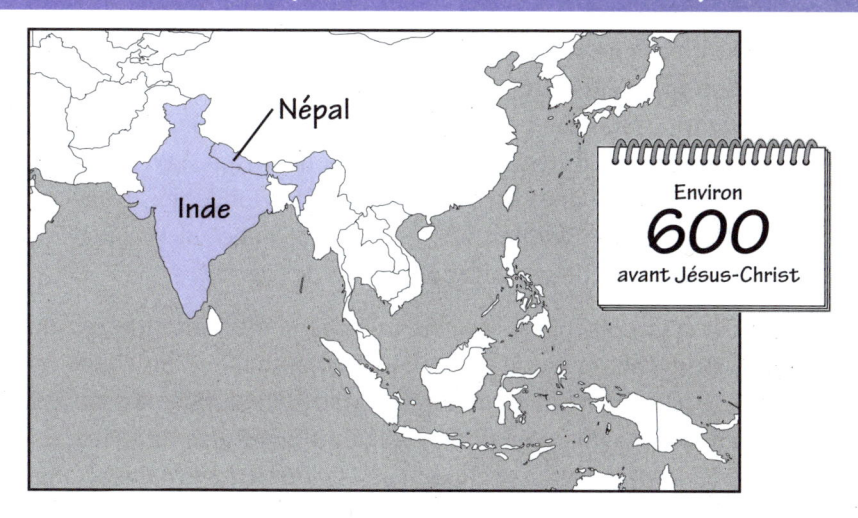

Environ
600
avant Jésus-Christ

Qui est le Bouddha ?

En langue sanskrite, le mot « bouddha » veut dire : « éveillé ». Les bouddhas sont donc des sages qui ont atteint une paix intérieure totale et permanente, grâce au détachement.

l existe de nombreux bouddhas en Inde et ailleurs dans le monde. Mais le plus connu est Siddhartha Gautama, le fondateur du bouddhisme, le premier homme à avoir été

« éveillé ». Il a vécu, environ 600 ans avant Jésus-Christ, à la frontière de l'Inde et du Népal.

Les récits de la vie du Bouddha se sont transmis par la tradition orale et ont été mis par écrit, pour la première fois, plusieurs centaines d'années après sa mort. Nous connaissons aujourd'hui différents types de bouddhisme, avec chacun leur manière de présenter la vie de leur fondateur. L'histoire de la vie de Siddhartha Gautama est donc un mélange de faits réels et de légendes porteuses de sagesse.

Selon ces légendes, sa mère aurait été mise enceinte par un petit éléphant blanc à six défenses, au cours d'un songe où elle fut pénétrée au côté droit. Quand elle donna naissance à un fils, les divinités firent pleuvoir des pétales de fleurs sur elle. L'enfant serait sorti de l'aisselle de sa mère, sans aucune douleur. Il se serait immédiatement tenu debout et aurait « pris possession » du monde, en se tournant vers les quatre points cardinaux (nord, sud, est, ouest). Cette entrée prodigieuse dans la vie annonçait déjà sa mission.

Le père de Siddhartha était le roi de la région. Les sages prédirent que son fils serait soit un grand roi, soit un grand maître spirituel. Il voulut absolument que son fils lui succède un jour. Il s'arrangea pour que Siddahartha passe son enfance dans l'enceinte du palais familial, protégé de toute souffrance.

Comment Siddhartha est-il devenu le Bouddha ?

À 29 ans, Siddhartha demanda à son père la permission d'aller se promener hors du palais. Il y fit quatre rencontres qui changèrent sa vie. Un vieillard, d'abord, lui fit découvrir la souffrance causée par la vieillesse. Puis un malade lui apprit la souffrance de la maladie. La vue d'un cadavre que l'on menait au bûcher, ensuite, lui révéla la douleur de la mort. Enfin, la rencontre d'un moine en méditation lui enseigna une façon de chercher la libération de la souffrance.

Comme il avait été protégé de tous ces malheurs, depuis son enfance, Siddhartha fut bouleversé par ces expériences. Il quitta le palais de son père, abandonna ses richesses et sa famille, pour entreprendre une vie nouvelle. Il commença par suivre les enseignements de plusieurs moines et adopta la méditation et le jeûne comme mode de vie. Pendant six ans, il ne mange presque rien et faillit mourir de faim. Il décida alors de trouver une autre façon d'atteindre son but.

Il accepta un bol de riz, ce qui lui donna la force de se concentrer sur la méditation. Il découvrit que « la voie moyenne », celle qui se situe entre les excès, est celle qui peut mener à la vérité.

Il s'installa alors sous un arbre. C'était une sorte de figuier, appelé aujourd'hui *bodhi*, ce qui veut dire : « arbre de l'éveil ». Il fit le vœu de ne pas bouger de là avant d'avoir atteint la vérité. C'est là qu'il atteint l'éveil ou l'illumination, et qu'il devint le Bouddha. Il comprenait désormais tous les mystères de la vie. Il partit donc pour enseigner aux autres ce qu'il venait de découvrir.

> Le lieu sacré le plus important pour le bouddhisme est un figuier *bodhi* qui serait un descendant de l'arbre sous lequel Siddhartha aurait atteint l'éveil. Des pèlerins bouddhistes s'y rendent pour tenter de vivre à leur tour l'expérience de Siddharta.

22

Quel est l'enseignement transmis par le Bouddha ?

Après son éveil, le Bouddha fit un premier discours dans lequel il révéla les quatre nobles vérités qui deviendront les fondements du bouddhisme.

La première vérité est que la souffrance fait partie de la vie.

La deuxième explique que la souffrance vient du désir. Par exemple, l'absence d'une personne que l'on aime rend triste, puisque l'on souhaite l'avoir à ses côtés.

La troisième vérité affirme que pour faire cesser la souffrance, il faut arrêter de désirer. Il faut donc se détacher de tout et contrôler ses désirs.

Enfin, la quatrième vérité enseigne la méthode menant à la libération, appelée « sentier du milieu » ou « noble sentier octuple ». Voici les huit principes du chemin vers l'éveil : la pensée juste, la compréhension juste, la parole juste, l'action juste, le travail juste, l'effort juste, l'attention juste et la concentration juste.

> Chacun des fondateurs abordés dans ce livre a vécu une expérience spirituelle qu'il a voulu partager avec les autres. Le Bouddha, tout comme Jésus, deviendra un guide pour les personnes qui voudront suivre son chemin spirituel.

Pourquoi des statues du Bouddha le représentent-elles gros et rieur ?

Selon la légende, Siddhartha Gautama aurait passé plusieurs années de sa vie pratiquement sans manger et qu'il serait presque mort de faim. Ces représentations d'un gros Bouddha rieur sont donc très étonnantes, pour nous. En réalité, elles proviennent de Chine. Ce pays est devenu bouddhiste plusieurs centaines d'années après la mort de Siddharta. Sa manière de vivre le bouddhisme est donc sensiblement différente de celle qui se vit en Inde. En fait, les statues chinoises du gros Bouddha rieur ne représentent pas Siddhartha Gautama, mais servent à illustrer la générosité, la richesse et l'abondance. Comme le ventre est considéré comme le lieu des émotions dans le corps, le gros ventre signifie un grand cœur. Les statues de Siddhartha Gautama provenant d'autres pays, comme l'Inde, ne le montrent jamais gros et souriant, mais plutôt dans une posture de méditation. Certaines de ces statues sont immenses. Elles représentent la stabilité nécessaire pour atteindre l'éveil.

24

GURU NANAK

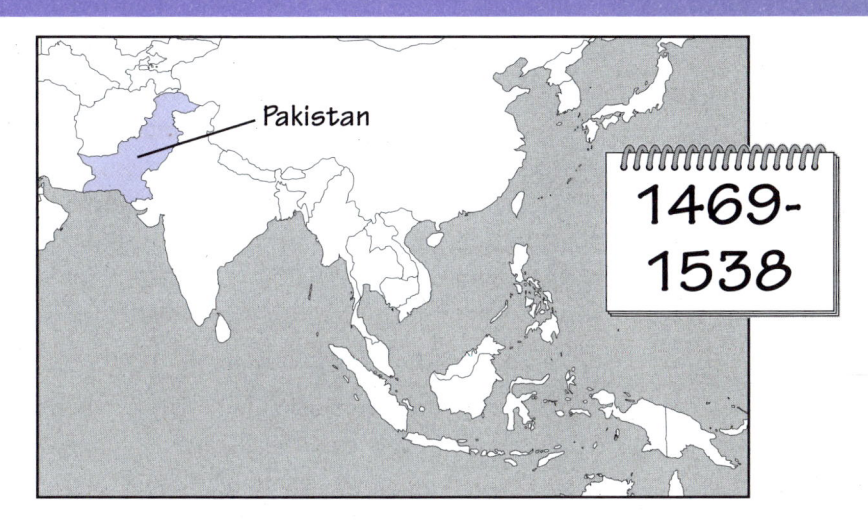

Pakistan

1469-1538

Qui est le fondateur de la religion des hommes coiffés d'un turban ?

Les hommes qui portent le turban, chez nous, sont des sikhs, des adeptes d'une religion appelée le sikhisme. *Sikh* veut dire : « disciple », en sanskrit, une très ancienne langue de l'Inde. Les sikhs sont les disciples du Guru (maître) Nanak.

25 Questions junior Les fondateurs

Le nom *Nanak* signifie : « sans nez », ce qui veut dire que Guru Nanak n'était pas centré sur sa personne, qu'il n'était pas égoïste.

Il a vécu de 1469 à 1538, dans une région du Pakistan. Ses parents étaient des marchands, adeptes de l'hindouisme, qu'ils ont transmis à leur fils. Mais Nanak avait un ami, Mardana, qui était musulman. Il l'accompagna dans son pèlerinage à La Mecque, en Arabie, et visita de nombreux pays : la Perse, l'Afghanistan, le Népal, le Tibet, l'Inde et le Sri Lanka.

Quand il rentra chez lui, il fonda une communauté et il y enseigna qu'il n'y a qu'un seul vrai Dieu, selon la profession de foi de l'islam. Ce Dieu réside dans le cœur de chaque personne et il est aussi le Créateur infiniment grand. De cette façon, il contestait le culte fait aux multiples divinités hindoues.

Quand il parle de Dieu, Guru Nanak utilise le mot *Vahiguru*, qui signifie : « le merveilleux maître », dans la langue punjabi.

Toute sa vie, Guru Nanak travaillera à l'union des hindous et des musulmans. La communauté qu'il fonde n'est ni hindoue ni musulmane, elle est sikh, c'est-à-dire : constituée de « disciples ».

Il lutte pour l'égalité entre les humains et contre les discriminations ou les préjugés liés à la race, la religion, le statut social. Il se fait le défenseur du droit des femmes à l'égalité, dans une société et une culture où elles étaient considérées comme inférieures.

Il est à l'origine d'une tradition musicale bien particulière, le *shabad kirtan*. Son enseignement a été mis en musique, sous forme d'hymnes et de poèmes. Le *adi granth* est la compilation de ses écrits poétiques qui sont chantés régulièrement dans les temples sikhs.

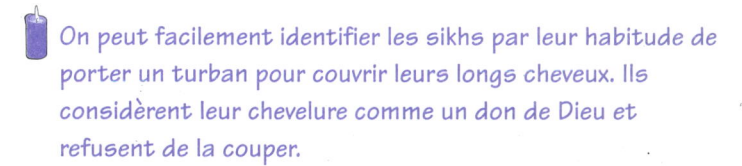

> On peut facilement identifier les sikhs par leur habitude de porter un turban pour couvrir leurs longs cheveux. Ils considèrent leur chevelure comme un don de Dieu et refusent de la couper.

> Ils doivent aussi porter le kirpan, un poignard décoratif. Celui-ci rappelle que les sikhs ont été victimes de persécutions et qu'ils doivent défendre leur liberté religieuse et celle de tous ceux qui sont opprimés.

Y a-t-il des religions sans fondateur?

Oui, il y a sur la terre plusieurs religions pour lesquelles nous ne connaissons pas de fondateur. Ce sont les plus anciennes et il est difficile de déterminer quand elles sont apparues, puisqu'elles sont nées avant l'invention de l'écriture. Elles se sont transmises oralement et à travers toutes sortes de rites et de coutumes, pendant des milliers d'années. Voici deux exemples de ces systèmes de croyances sans fondateur : les spiritualités amérindiennes et l'hindouisme.

LES SPIRITUALITÉS AMÉRINDIENNES

Environ **3000** avant Jésus-Christ

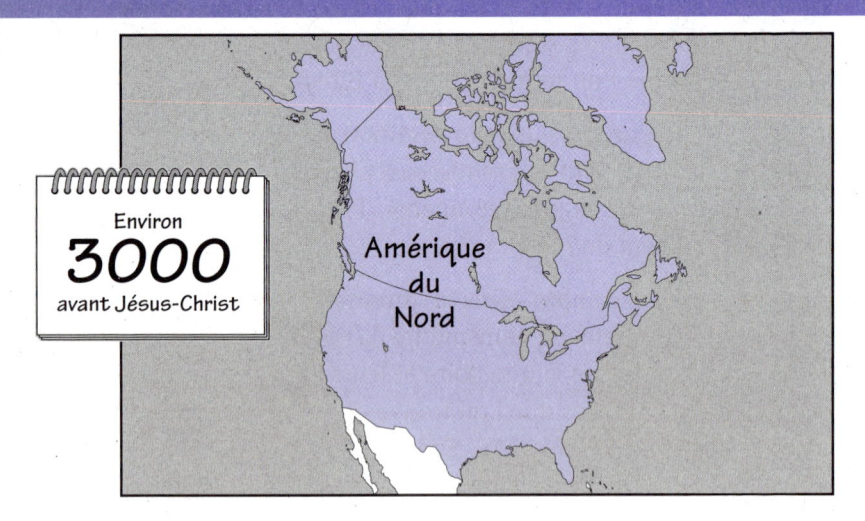

Amérique du Nord

Les nations amérindiennes sont apparues en Amérique, il y a plusieurs millénaires. La transmission de leur sagesse s'est faite oralement, à travers des légendes et des récits racontés aux plus jeunes. Comme il y a une grande diversité de nations amérindiennes, il y a une grande diversité de croyances. Mais il est possible de faire ressortir certains de leurs points communs.

Les Amérindiens croient dans l'ensemble en un Dieu créateur. Celui-ci est souvent appelé « le Grand Esprit » (« Manitou », pour les Algonquins). Des « esprits », bons ou mauvais, sont associés aux animaux ou aux phénomènes naturels.

Pour eux, la nature est sacrée. Certains lieux, comme une montagne, un lac, un arbre, un rocher, sont habités par des forces surnaturelles. Ils sont le site de grandes cérémonies : funérailles, initiations, visions, etc. Le respect de la nature est une valeur essentielle pour eux et, grâce à eux, nous la redécouvrons aujourd'hui.

Les différentes nations amérindiennes partagent aussi certains rites, par exemple : la loge à transpirer pour se purifier, les *pow-wow*, ces rassemblements festifs accompagnés de musiques et de danses traditionnelles. Les rituels religieux comportent des prières en cercle, des danses et des offrandes à la Terre mère.

Aujourd'hui, la majorité des Amérindiens sont chrétiens. Mais certains tentent de retrouver leur véritable identité, en remettant à l'honneur des coutumes et des rites d'autrefois.

L'HINDOUISME

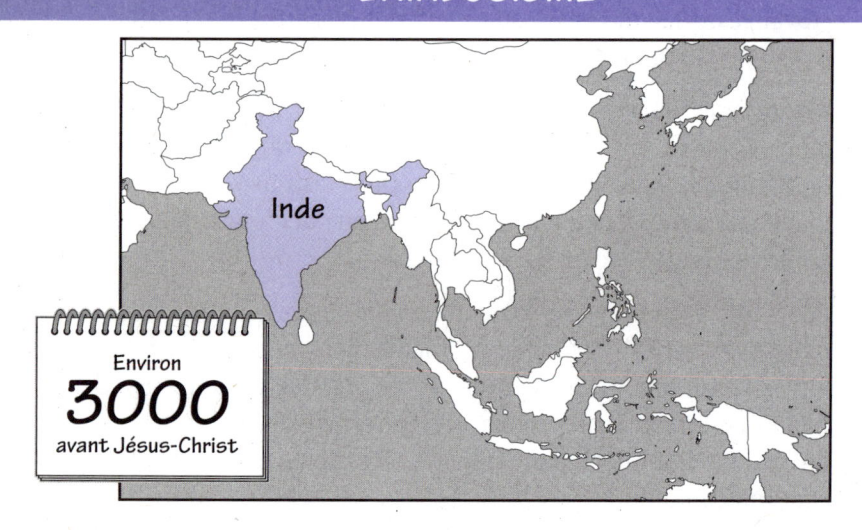

Environ **3000** avant Jésus-Christ

La civilisation indienne est très ancienne, elle remonte à 3000 ans avant Jésus-Christ. À l'origine de l'hindouisme, on retrouve un mélange de croyances et de pratiques religieuses des habitants de l'Inde. L'hindouisme n'a pas de fondateur véritable parce qu'on n'y trouve pas de personnage central ayant mission d'enseigner une vérité. Mais c'est une tradition riche de trois mille ans de cultures et de spiritualités qui s'entrecroisent.

Les livres sacrés de l'hindouisme constituent une véritable bibliothèque : Vedas, Mahabharata, Bhagavad Gita et Ramayana. Ces textes racontent les grands mythes de la tradition hindoue. Ils ont été écrits sur une longue période allant de 1500 ans avant Jésus-Christ à 500 ans après Jésus-Christ. On y découvre une façon de voir la vie très différente de la nôtre.

L'un des concepts clés de cette foi est la réincarnation. Selon cette théorie, les humains doivent vivre des renaissances successives pour se libérer de leurs faiblesses. Leur bonheur ne consiste donc pas en une vie après la mort, mais, au contraire, en la fin des réincarnations. Ils ont alors atteint le *nirvana*, le bonheur suprême.

L'hindouisme se différencie aussi des grandes traditions religieuses par son grand nombre de dieux. On en compte plus de trois mille ! Les plus importants sont : Brahman (l'Infini), Vishnou (la protection), Shiva (la destruction), Krishna (l'amour), Râma (la perfection), Hanuman (la bravoure) et Ganesha (le dieu à tête d'éléphant qui écarte les obstacles).

Si l'hindouisme n'a pas de fondateur, il compte pourtant de grandes figures. Il suffit de penser à Mohandas Karamchand

Gandhi (1869-1948), un dirigeant politique et un guide spirituel important de l'Inde. Son surnom, Mahatma, veut dire : « grande âme ». Il a lutté pour l'indépendance de son pays et il est reconnu partout dans le monde comme un homme de paix. Au lieu d'utiliser la violence pour faire des changements sociaux, il a choisi la résistance passive et le jeûne. Toute sa vie, il a lutté pour les droits des femmes et contre toute forme d'exclusion. Il a été assassiné, alors qu'il se rendait à une réunion de prière.

TABLEAU SYNTHÈSE

Pour résumer notre parcours, voici un tableau rassemblant différentes informations sur les fondateurs dont nous avons parlé.

FONDATEURS	RELIGIONS	DATES	PAYS	LIVRES	CARACTÉRISTIQUES
Abraham	judaïsme	environ – 1800	Canaan (Israël)	Bible (Genèse)	Père des religions monothéistes.
Moïse	judaïsme	environ – 1300	Égypte	Bible (Exode)	Libérateur du peuple hébreu; transmetteur des dix commandements.
David	judaïsme	environ – 1000	Israël	Bible (Roi, Samuel, Chroniques)	Roi d'Israël; auteur présumé des psaumes.
Jésus	christianisme	de 0 à 33	Israël	Nouveau Testament	Mort et ressuscité; présenté comme le Messie, le Fils de Dieu.
Paul	christianisme	environ de 10 à 65	autour de la Méditerranée	Lettres de Paul Acte des Apôtres	Fondateur de communautés chrétiennes; auteur de lettres aux communautés.
Martin Luther	christianisme	1483-1546	Allemagne	Traduction de la Bible en allemand	Traducteur de la Bible; l'un des fondateurs du protestantisme.
Muhammad	islam	570-632	Arabie	Coran	Prophète d'Allah; auteur du Coran.
Siddhartha Gautama Le Bouddha	bouddhisme	environ – 600	Inde et Népal	Les suttas, en pali, transmettent ses discours	Le grand « éveillé », enseignant.
Guru Nanak	sikhisme	1469-1538	Pakistan	Adi Granth	Défenseur de l'unicité de Dieu; défenseur de l'égalité de tous.
Aucun	hindouisme	environ – 3000	Inde	Veda, Mahabharata, Bhagavad Gita et Ramayana	Plusieurs dieux; croyance en la réincarnation.
Aucun	religion amérindienne	environ – 3000	Amérique du Nord	aucun	Respect religieux de la nature.

25 Questions junior Les fondateurs

MÉDIAGRAPHIE POUR LES ENFANTS

Pour plus d'informations, tu peux consulter les outils suivants :

Livres :

La collection « Labyrinthes », aux Éditions La Pensée inc., Montréal : *La tradition chrétienne*, *La tradition bouddhiste*, *La tradition hindoue*, *La tradition juive*, *Le phénomène religieux* et *Le guide des grandes religions*.

La collection « Témoins en herbes », Les Réalisatout, Éditions Novalis, Montréal : *Vivre le grand départ*, *Traverser les miroirs*, *Choisir son port d'attache*, *S'apprivoiser à la différence*, *Voir grandeur nature*, *Amadouer le dragon*, *S'ouvrir au mystère*.

Sites Internet :

Le portail des religions du site Vikidia, L'encyclopédie francophone pour les 8 à 13 ans :
http://fr.vikidia.org/index.php/Portail:Religions

Le christianisme, l'islam et le judaïsme expliqués aux enfants :
http://decouvrelesreligions.free.fr/

MÉDIAGRAPHIE POUR LES PARENTS

Pour plus d'informations, nous vous proposons de consulter :

Sites Internet :

Dans l'encyclopédie collective Wikipédia, le portail Théopédia est consacré aux religions et croyances et contient beaucoup de liens et de renseignements :

http://fr.wikipedia.org/wiki/Portail:Théopédia

Pour mieux connaître la Bible, voir :

www.interbible.org

Pour des commentaires sur les textes bibliques utilisés dans les célébrations eucharistiques, afin de faciliter la réflexion des enfants, voir :

http://www.liturgie-enfants.com

Pour une introduction à l'islam, et pour lire et entendre le Coran en ligne :

http://islamfrance.free.fr/coran.html

TABLE DES MATIÈRES

Mot de l'auteur 3

ABRAHAM
1. Qui était Abraham ? 4
2. Pourquoi dit-on qu'Abraham est le père des juifs, des chrétiens et des musulmans ? 6

MOÏSE
3. Est-ce que Moïse est le fondateur de la religion juive ? 8
4. Que veut dire le nom de Moïse ? 9
5. Comment Moïse a-t-il rencontré Dieu ? 11
6. Moïse réussira-t-il à libérer son peuple ? 12
7. Comment Moïse a-t-il reçu les dix commandements ? 15

DAVID
8. Quels sont les autres grands noms du judaïsme ? 18

JÉSUS DE NAZARETH
9. Pourquoi fête-t-on la naissance de Jésus à Noël ? 21
10. Pourquoi parle-t-on encore de Jésus aujourd'hui ? ... 24
11. Pourquoi Jésus a-t-il fait des miracles ? 26

12. Que veut-on dire quand on affirme que Jésus
    est ressuscité ? 28
13. Pourquoi les chrétiens disent-ils que Jésus est
    à la fois homme et Dieu ? 29

PAUL DE TARSE
14. Qui est Paul de Tarse ? Comment a-t-il aidé
    le christianisme à grandir ? 31

MARTIN LUTHER
15. Tous les chrétiens sont-ils catholiques ?
    Qui est Martin Luther ? 34

MUHAMMAD
16. Qui est le fondateur de l'islam ? 37
17. Comment Allah (Dieu) a-t-il fait de Muhammad
    son messager ? 39
18. Comment se termine la vie de Muhammad ? 41
19. Pourquoi ne voit-on pas d'images de Muhammad
    ou très rarement ? 42

LE BOUDDHA (SIDDHARTA GAUTAMA)

20. Qui est le Bouddha? 43
21. Comment Siddharta Gautama est-il devenu le Bouddha? 45
22. Quel est l'enseignement transmis par le Bouddha? 46
23. Pourquoi des statues du Bouddha le représentent-elles gros et rieur? 48

GURU NANAK

24. Qui est le fondateur de la religion des hommes coiffés d'un turban? 49
25. Y a-t-il des religions sans fondateur? 52
    Les spiritualités amérindiennes 52
    L'hindouisme 54

Tableau synthèse 57

Médiagraphie pour les enfants 58

Médiagraphie pour les parents 59

certifié   procédé sans chlore   100% post-consommation   archives permanentes   énergie biogaz certifié   procédé sans chlore   100% post-consommation   archives permanentes   énergie biogaz

LE BOUDDHA (SIDDHARTA GAUTAMA)

20. Qui est le Bouddha? 43
21. Comment Siddharta Gautama est-il devenu le Bouddha? 45
22. Quel est l'enseignement transmis par le Bouddha? 46
23. Pourquoi des statues du Bouddha le représentent-elles gros et rieur? 48

GURU NANAK

24. Qui est le fondateur de la religion des hommes coiffés d'un turban? 49
25. Y a-t-il des religions sans fondateur? 52
    Les spiritualités amérindiennes 52
    L'hindouisme 54

Tableau synthèse 57

Médiagraphie pour les enfants 58

Médiagraphie pour les parents 59